The Insider's Guide to

Getting Your Book Published

The Insider's Guide to

Getting Your Book Published

Rachael Stock

Editors Richard Craze, Roni Jay

Viva Books

New Delhi | Mumbai | Chennai | Kolkata | Bangalore | Hyderabad | Kochi | Guwahati

First Indian Edition 2010

VIVA BOOKS PRIVATE LIMITED

- 4737/23 Ansari Road, Daryaganj, New Delhi 110 002
  E-mail: vivadelhi@vivagroupindia.net, Tel. 42242200
- 76, Service Industries, Shirvane, Sector 1, Nerul, Navi Mumbai 400 706
  E-mail: vivamumbai@vivagroupindia.net, Tel. 27721273, 27721274
- Jamals Fazal Chambers, 26 Greams Road, Chennai 600 006
  E-mail: vivachennai@vivagroupindia.net, Tel. 28290304, 28294241
- B-103, Jindal Towers, 21/1A/3 Darga Road, Kolkata 700 017
  E-mail: vivakolkata@vivagroupindia.net, Tel. 22836381, 22816713
- 7, Sovereign Park Apartments, 56-58, K. R. Road, Basavanagudi, Bangalore 560 004
  E-mail: vivabangalore@vivagroupindia.net, Tel. 26607409, 26607410
- 101-102 Mughal Marc Apartments, 3-4-637 to 641, Narayanguda, Hyderabad 500 029
  E-mail: vivahyderabad@vivagroupindia.net, Tel. 27564481, 27564482
- Beevi Towers, First Floor, SRM Road, Kaloor, Kochi 682 018, Kerala
  E-mail: vivakochi@vivagroupindia.net, Tel: 0484-2403055, 2403056
- 232, GNB Road, Beside UCO Bank, Silpukhuri, Guwahati 781 003
  E-mail: vivaguwahati@vivagroupindia.net, Tel: 0361-2666386

www.vivagroupindia.com

Published by arrangement with

Crimson Publishing,
a division of Crimson Business Ltd
Westminster House, Kew Road
Richmond, Surrey TW9 2ND

ISBN : 978-81-309-1491-6

Published by Vinod Vasishtha for Viva Books Private Limited, 4737/23, Ansari Road, Daryaganj, New Delhi - 110 002.

Printed and bound by Raj Press, R-3, Inderpuri, New Delhi - 110 012.

Contents

"They say everybody has a book in them. I managed to get mine out. I just hope nobody tries to put it back in again."

Guy Browning

Acknowledgements

One of the very many interesting experiences of being a publisher turned writer (probably for this book, and this book only) is that I've had to wrestle with not doing things as an author that irritate me as a publisher. Avoiding endless and tedious acknowledgements is one of these. This could be tough, but here goes:

Thank you Logan for being so noble and agreeing, without complaint, to go fishing for hours on end, every weekend, to give me peace to write. The sacrifice is noted. For evermore, you are right and I am sorry.

Huge thanks to Roni and Rich – my authors turned publishers. Our role reversal has been great fun – I've learned such a lot from you over the years, and had such a good time doing it. You're simply brilliant.

Thanks also to everybody who contributed to this book, with or without knowing it. Of the people I didn't know previously who were so helpful, a very special thank you to Emma Cahill, Helen Conford, Ian Jackson, Laura James and Antony Topping who have been particularly generous with their time and their views and are the kind of people who make publishing such a joy to be a part of.

Thanks to Steve Parks, Anna Smedgard and Nic Peeling for being guinea pig test readers and for their invaluable feedback.

I'd like to thank Pearson, for being genuinely such a great company to work for, from Marjorie and David at the top, through all the people too numerous to mention, to Richard my brilliant boss (how many people can say that?) and all the team I work with now.

The people I have learned most from over the years also need a mention – from the early days, John who first encouraged me to follow him into commissioning, Georgina and Sean who gave me my first break, and Rebecca and Nicky for relieving the occasional boredom of my desk editor apprenticeship. Emma and Kenny were the long suffering design partners with whom I fought endlessly over whether we should cut words or pictures, and Anna helped me with the case for the sanctity of words. And to the present, a special mention for Richard and Elie who are as wise as the day is long, and without whom I would be utterly lost. Plus of course my fantastic authors, from whom I've learned more than any of them could imagine, especially Carmel (my hero and friend).

And finally, to my mum and dad, for all your love and support.

(Was that brief enough? Gosh that was difficult…)

Introduction

Do you have a burning desire to write a book? Or have you already written it and just want to know how to get it published? Is it just this one particular book you are passionate about, or do you want to become a full time writer and need guidance on what to write and who to sell it to? Whatever your situation, the quest to get into print can seem an utterly daunting one. Unless of course you have an insider to guide you.

This book reveals how publishers operate, who makes the decisions, what influences them, how you can make you and your book instantly more appealing to an agent or publisher and how to create the brilliant submission that will shine amongst the pile of tired words on a commissioning editor's desk.

It also reveals what to do if you get a rejection (or 10) and, if you can't find a publisher who wants to take your book, or you don't like any of them, then you'll discover what your other options are, from using a publishing service to complete DIY self publishing.

We're assuming that you've got the kernel of a good idea (we'll test this as far as we can along the way) and that you can write, or are willing to work with somebody who can. However, many good writers and great books go unpublished. This is about making sure you and yours aren't among them.

In the same way that many good books don't make it to the shelves, plenty of books do get published but don't sell. This book is also about doing all you can to make sure that doesn't happen. In the process of constructing a brilliant pitch, you can usually pick out areas that might be weak, and either re-evaluate the proposal or the book to deal with it. This will make the project and the book more appealing to readers as well as to publishers. We'll also look at how you can work with a publisher to maximise the chances of your book selling well once published.

What's the secret?

Getting published is more a combination of art and luck than it is science. There is no single magic formula that will absolutely guarantee you success; however there are plenty of strategies that will vastly increase your chances of getting published. That's the 'art' bit and that's what this book is about.

Luck undoubtedly does play a part: the biggest hurdle in getting published is whether what you propose tickles the fancy of a single person – either an agent or an editor. And that in turn depends on that person's personal preferences, their experience, what they happen to be looking for at that time, their gut feelings and possibly even whether they got out of bed the right side that morning (if we're being really honest).

However, getting the right book, explained in the right way, in front of the right person isn't all luck – far from it. This book will show you how you make sure you do just that.

What kind of book?

Obviously, there are many different types of publisher and many styles of publishing. Not everything in this book will apply to all genres or categories, but there are a surprising number of commonalities. Different attributes are needed for a good children's book as opposed to a good history book or business book or novel. However, the principles of how publishers work, the process of choosing and approaching a publisher or agent, and the crafting of a winning submission are pretty similar. Sometimes advice applies particularly to fiction or non-fiction, and I've tried to flag clearly where this is the case, but the best advice is that you read with a filter of 'does this apply to my book?' running in your head. Discard whatever doesn't seem to apply, and just pick up on what does.

Most existing general books on getting published are biased towards fiction rather than non-fiction, yet there's a lot more to be said about how you submit non-fiction ideas (ie the pitch as opposed to the sample text itself). I've tried to find a balance between the two and hope I've succeeded.

First things first

A huge number of people have an idea for a book at some point in their lives. Though writing a book is simple in theory (after all, you only need a computer, or pen and paper), very few people have an idea, sit down and write a good book, just like that. Writing is a craft, like painting or carving or anything else creative. Having the tools of the trade doesn't make you a master craftsman. This book is not about how to write – there are plenty of books on that subject already (see the reading list at **www.whiteladderpress.com**). Suffice to say here that I can't recommend highly enough that you read everything you can about the art of writing well, do a course and practise, practise, practise. To succeed, it is likely that you'll need to invest a lot of time and effort into the project.

A very important golden rule

However good the tips in this book, if you write badly in style, sense, structure or content, you won't get published.

As well as doing a lot of practice writing, you should also do a lot of reading. As one agent said to me, "Wide ranging, absorbent readers make better writers."

We're going to assume from here on that what you have written, or are thinking of writing, is fit for publication – but I urge you to learn your craft, learn it well and practise until your hands are sore before you set out on the journey towards getting published.

The insider's view

As the book title suggests, I am an insider. I've been a commissioning editor for over 12 years, with three different companies, and have published illustrated and non-illustrated books on health, medicine, sport, natural history, the outdoors, popular psychology, history, religion, personal development, business, science and even the odd bit of fiction. (One possibly unintentionally, but that's another story.) In this book I'll be telling you how it is from 'the other side' – what leaps off the desk and what goes straight into the bin. However, I knew from the outset that my own experience was not enough for this book to be as useful as it possibly could be to all aspiring unpublished authors. So I have interviewed as broad a range of other editors, agents, published authors and senior people from all kinds of publishing houses as possible, in order to check that my views were not personal quirks. In fact, I have been rather surprised just how much my experiences and beliefs tallied with those of people who commission in very different areas, and whom I have never met. It's worth saying however that no two agents, editors or publishers are the same, hence there are sometimes two views on the same issue, and this is reflected in the book.

Some of the agents, editors and authors I interviewed said they would rather remain anonymous – either generally or in relation to specific quotes, views or anecdotes. I have therefore honoured this. It's sometimes the only way to tell it how it really is. However, every story or quote in this book is completely genuine. I'm far too scrupulous to make things up.

This is by no means an exhaustive guide to the publishing industry and everything you might possibly need to know about writing and publishing. It's really an 'essentials of' – a quick and dirty guide rather than an encyclopaedia. My aim has been to flag the key things I find most first time authors don't know, that would really enhance their publishing prospects if they did, and to cover the basics of how the process works.

Like most commissioning editors, I've published international bestsellers, and I have published a few real dogs. Publishing is like that. On a daily basis, I've received proposals that made me sigh, proposals that made me laugh, proposals that made me angry and proposals that delighted and excited me. My aim in writing this book is to make sure that your submission falls firmly in that last category.

I'd be delighted to hear from you with feedback and suggestions – drop me a line at **rachael@stockanderson.com**. Here's to your great success!

1 How books are commissioned

An insider's guide to the process of publishing

Though publishers like to distinguish themselves from other companies (witness the term 'publishing house'), when it comes down to it almost all are, as you would expect, commercial enterprises. As such they are looking to make a profit. Even the University Presses make most of their decisions about what to publish on a commercial basis.

Getting your book published usually means convincing a number of people who work for the publisher that your book will make them money. This might sound like stating the obvious but you'd be surprised how many aspiring authors forget or ignore this when pitching to a publisher.

> "All you publishers are obsessed about whether or not it will sell."
> *Would-be author to publisher, when asked if the proposed book was practical*

There are of course other considerations – most, but not all, publishers want to have a list of titles that they are proud of, so quality should count too. But the bottom line is the bottom line. Which means that what you are effectively trying to do is persuade a group of people that they will be able to sell enough copies of your book to make them a healthy profit – ideally without causing them too much strain along the way. We'll come back to how you actually do this in detail later on. It's sufficient here that you know that the decision making process is unlikely to be one person thinking that this is a rather nice idea that deserves to see the light of day. It's very likely that the hard headed senior sales people and even the bean counters have their say.

Here then are the key steps in getting a book published:

1 Your proposal arrives on the desk of the commissioning editor, either directly or via an agent.

2 The commissioning editor then either rejects the proposal, or comes back to you to discuss the book.

3 When the commissioning editor is happy, they present the book concept and costings to a group of key decision makers (here we'll call it a publishing committee – different publishers use different names).

4 The publishing committee (usually including sales people, marketing and publicity people, foreign rights people, senior management and others – even finance directors) discuss all aspects of the book and reach a conclusion as to whether or not they should take on the book for publication.

5 The commissioning editor comes back to you with either an offer of a contract or a rejection.

This is of course extremely simplified – there are lots of variables in every step and all publishers are slightly different. However, this serves as a rough guide as to how the average medium to large publisher works.

Very rarely it can be extraordinarily simple – your proposal is staggeringly brilliant and original and just what the commissioning editor is looking for (or of course you are an A list celebrity, which always helps) in which case the process above gets condensed into one phone call, a quick word with the boss and the offer is on the table within the hour. At the other end of the spectrum, just step 1 alone can require all the guile and persistence you possess and even if you do make it, the next step can take six months or more while the commissioning editor shilly shallies around, deliberates, blows hot and cold and finally leaves the company so you have to start all over again.

Profit and pride

I am very much aware that many authors, especially those trying to get published for the first time, are appalled by publishers' focus on profit, apparently at the expense of an appreciation of literary merit or the worthiness of the subject. I guess what I would say is this: publishers are businesses, and most are accountable to shareholders or investors, or at the very least have to produce enough profit to provide a living for the owner and staff. It is a business like any other. However this said, the amount of emphasis placed on the importance of literary merit and quality varies enormously from publisher to publisher. It's worth digging below the surface to find out where potential publishers stand in the spectrum.

More importantly still, remember that though the publisher as a company clearly will have a focus on the bottom line, the individual commissioning editor you are appealing to is an interesting mix of businessperson and creative. Most editors don't do it for the money (publishing doesn't pay terribly well on the whole). Their drive is often the thrill of working with brilliant writers and developing great concepts. There are thankfully few editors who really don't care about the quality of what they publish, so long as it makes a profit. So if you are tempted to despair at the ever greater commercialisation of publishing, remember that somewhere in the corporate behemoth is a human being who is excited by brilliant writing. The challenge is getting to one who is excited by you.

On this point, it's worth always keeping in mind that one person's joy is another's boredom. What works for one doesn't always work for another. Which is why you should never assume because one editor doesn't like what you've done, that all will feel the same way.

One thing you should always remember however:

Golden rule

The editor is interested in what people want to read, not what you want to write.

It's worth thinking hard about this. It's very easy to assume that because you want to write it, that's all that matters. Are you sure you are writing what people want to read?

Getting to the desk

There are two main ways of getting to the commissioning editor's desk: directly, or indirectly via an agent. Some publishers are happy to accept unsolicited proposals, which means that they will look at ideas direct from authors (published or unpublished) and will consider speculative submissions. Other publishers will deal only with agents and won't consider anything sent in by a would-be author. Broadly speaking, non-fiction publishers tend to be more open to unsolicited proposals, and fiction publishers are more likely to work via agents only. The main reason for this is that the sheer number of people who send in fiction, the vast majority of which won't make the grade for publication, makes it completely impossible for the publisher to read all of them. That's where agents come in – they act as a kind of filter and direct projects with potential to the right kind of publisher. Many authors believe it's much harder to find an agent than a publisher, for fiction. We'll look at what agents do, how they operate, and – critically – whether or not you need one, in Chapter 4. There is a number of small publishers who do look at unsolicited fiction however. It's not an absolute rule.

We've assumed so far that the trick is getting your proposal to the desk – it's your idea in search of a publisher. In non-fiction, sometimes it does work the other way, and the publisher has an idea they need to find an author to write. If you have a specific idea, it still might be worth trying to get on a publisher's radar this way, as while you are talking about the book project they have in mind, you can get yours on the table too.

Actually there is a slight irony here. At the same time as thousands of writers desperate to have their book published are sitting staring dejectedly at rejection slips (or waiting in vain for the phone to ring), there are groups of people in publishing companies across the capital and beyond desperately trying to think up new ideas for books (non-fiction, clearly). This shows that there are publishers who would be delighted if you could present them with something they would want to publish. Right concept, right time, right publisher, right pitch – bingo. It is that simple, and then of course, it isn't as you don't know what's going on in the mind of the commissioning editor…

Inside the mind of the commissioning editor

The commissioning editor (also known as acquisitions editor, editor, senior editor or publisher) is the first and most important person in the publishing company as far as you are concerned. If the proposal never gets to the right person, clearly you're not going to get published. If you don't convince the commissioning editor that your book should be published, it won't be published. The commissioning editor isn't likely to be the sole decision maker, as we've seen above, but they are your advocate, your representative within the company. They will act for you and persuade and influence and pitch internally on your behalf. If they love you and what you are proposing, then you've got the very best chance of getting that elusive publishing contract. For that reason we'll look at who they are and what turns them on (and switches them right off) and how you can get them to want you.

The first rule of influencing is of course 'know thy target'. Commissioning editors do vary enormously in personality, from the introvert to the extrovert, from the literary enthusiast and subject specialist to the extremely commercially minded and sometimes less quality focused. But there are some general commonalities. The first thing to know is that they have probably worked really hard to get where they are and endured hugely tedious jobs along the way. Commissioning is fiercely competitive. Most have served a long apprenticeship either as an editorial assistant (generally a slightly glorified secretarial/admin role), as a desk editor (copyediting, proofreading, and generally wielding a red pen, or managing freelancers who do the hands on work) or as a sales rep or marketing assistant. Unless they have been hired solely for their subject knowledge, their amassed wisdom about the publishing business is usually pretty good. It's a powerful job; the commissioning editor is usually the hub of the whole operation.

The best commissioning editors have a very finely tuned gut instinct as to what will work and what won't. They use it a lot. They have to balance what they like with commercial considerations – and when the two are as one, it makes them very happy. Editors get a real buzz out of discovering new talent and publishing a book they really love. Taking on a book they believe in and seeing it sell in huge quantities is publishing nirvana.

However editors can be tormented souls. There's sometimes a nagging fear they may be rejecting the big one. The bestseller they didn't spot. On a daily basis, there's the ever present possibility that they will be the person who rejected Harry Potter or turned down *Eats, Shoots and Leaves.* When you're working largely on market awareness and gut instinct, there's plenty of room for error.

> **Insider's view**
>
> At my very best, I can pick five projects to commission, and be pretty confident that three will be successful. But I can't tell you which three. And I don't think I am ever going to achieve better odds than that. There are too many variables, and it's too unpredictable.
>
> A very senior publishing director at a different publisher told a new editor recently that if she got a 60% hit rate, she was doing well, which tallies with my 'three from five.'

I sometimes think that what authors don't realise is that some books can mean almost as much to the editor as they do to the author. They are proud of them, they care terribly about what people say about them, they have a sense of ownership of the books and responsibility for them. If they don't sell well, it can really get under the editor's skin. Ideally, you want an editor who will care this much about your book.

Four essential rules for dealing with commissioning editors

1 Be confident but not bossy

Show that you are very positive and sure of your project and your market. Don't tell them their job or suggest you know better than they do. Upbeat but slightly deferential tends to go down well: 'I firmly believe this book will appeal to the 100,000 horse owners in the UK and will fill the gap below *Exhaustive Horse Care*, but I'm aware I do need your expert guidance as to whether I've pitched the book at exactly the right level for the biggest audience, and settled on the most suitable format.'

2 Do your research

A covering letter that includes a reference to their earlier publishing achievements will always be well received: 'I saw the acknowledgement to you in Ken Smith's *Illustrated History of The Second World War*, a book I've always admired, and really wanted you to be the first person I approached with my book proposal.'

3 Be likeable

All commissioning editors have a few nightmare authors they have to work with because their books sell well. And they do it through absolutely gritted teeth. But they are human beings and would so much rather work with somebody they think will be interesting and fun to work with. For borderline projects, this could be the deciding factor. Never ever be aggressive or terse or arrogant. Don't go over their heads. Even if you are really frustrated with them. Be positive, understanding and helpful.

4 Tread carefully the fine line between pest and persistent

Commissioning editors are very busy people. Stuff drops off the edges. They know this and often feel really guilty. The art is encouraging them to respond without making them feel so negative about you that your proposal goes in the bin. A voicemail rant expressing your real dissatisfaction at not hearing back from them for two weeks doesn't go down half as well as a short email that says how you really are sorry to ask as you know they are probably really besieged by proposals, but you just wondered if they had had a chance to look at it yet as you are really looking forward to their reaction.

The above applies to most agents also.

The more you can understand the mind of the editor or agent, the more likely you are to be successful. I guess the best way I can describe it to you is this. Next time you pick up a new book off the shelf, or read about it on amazon or described somewhere, and you feel really excited by the prospect of buying that book and taking it home – that's how it feels to be an editor when they find a great project. Next time you open a book and start to read and it delights you, captures you, you can't put it down – that's how it feels to be an agent reading a manuscript that works for them for the very first time. Next time you have those experiences as a browser, as a reader, hold on to them and think very hard about why the book has made you feel that way. These are the feelings you need to evoke in your target person when you make your submission.

At this point you may well be thinking: 'hang on, the book I want to write is a book about starting a business or making furniture out of junk. I can understand why you would get that reaction if you'd sent in a great novel, but surely that doesn't apply to my book?' You might be surprised. Unless the editor hates their job, or regards it as something to pay the mortgage (unlikely in publishing) they will derive happiness from a good submission. It's a pleasure to read something well thought out and well written. Even if it isn't a potential Booker prize winner, it lifts the spirits to come across something in which you can see the commercial potential. Either way you want to make the editor excited – either about the quality or about the number of copies they think they can sell. Preferably both.

What do commissioning editors want?

Ah. The 64 thousand dollar question. Here's the short answer. All that commissioning editors are looking for is:

- a book idea that appeals to them,
- that fits their list,
- that they can pitch easily to their colleagues,
- that will sell loads of copies,
- that they will be proud to publish, and
- that will make them look fantastic.
- Oh and somebody that they will really enjoy working with.

Not much then really.

A commissioning editor normally has a 'list' which is the imprint and/or subject areas they commission in. It's very important to send your proposal to the right person in charge of the right list, as there is no guarantee that if it goes to the wrong person they will pass it on. The most common rejection phrase is probably 'I'm afraid it doesn't fit the list' or 'I don't see a place for this in my list'. Sometimes, yes, this is a catch-all excuse for not providing a proper answer, because the book proposal is just unattractive generally, but it can be true. If a book doesn't fit in terms of subject area you are obviously not going to be accepted, but this can equally apply to the approach or style of the book. Like any other business, publishers and their lists are 'brands' and will have brand values. For example, two cookery publishers might be at the opposite ends of the scale – one might only do lavish highly illustrated books while another might specialise in small, cheap cookbooks.

Golden rule

Spend the time researching the lists you are interested in. You can usually see what kinds of book a commissioning editor is going to go for if you put in some time and effort.

Usually, it's a combination of originality and yet 'fit' that an editor is looking for. Ian Jackson, the wise Editorial Director of illustrated book packager Eddison Sadd, has a useful analogy for the holy grail of publishing, "It's like surfing. You've got to catch that wave. You've got to be agile and quick, ready to stand up at exactly the right time. You don't want to miss a wave completely; to watch others publish and think 'how did I miss that?' Equally you don't want to get on it and fall off immediately, because you hadn't got it right. And then there's the chance you will ride the wave for a short distance and then you can't keep up, because for example you ran out of stock at the critical time."

As a writer, you need to be able to judge the waves too. Get on them at the right time and you're more likely to get published and make a publisher very happy. Too early, and the market won't be ready. Too late and you'll be looking at me-too publishing.

> "Don't mistake a hearse for a bandwagon."
> *Richard Stagg, Editorial Director, Pearson Education*

As a publisher, it's very tempting when you've had or seen success with a particular book to want to do more in the same vein. And it can work – you see this all the time with trends like 'chick lit' or the surge in property makeover books, or even a big rise in sales of a particular genre: romantic novels, for example, whose sales revenue nearly doubled in the three years to 2004. However, you need to be looking ahead constantly for the next big thing.

> "Remember that the 'new' books you see in a bookstore were actually commissioned up to two years ago."
> *Antony Topping, Agent, Greene & Heaton Ltd*

For publishers – and therefore for smart authors – it's about finding a careful balance between providing what readers want and capitalising on expanding areas of interest, and in starting new trends. It's very easy to be so absorbed in publishing or writing one area to death that you forget to look up and see what else might be on the horizon.

Successful authors, like successful publishers and agents, tend to be good at spotting what's next.

Golden rule

It's extremely important when thinking about your book idea to look at the market and judge if your book is one whose time is coming, or whose time has passed.

That's not to say there isn't a place for me-too publishing, and commissioning editors know this. Although we don't call it that of course. There's often room for doing something that's been done before, but doing it better. Most would agree it's folly to ignore a big, lucrative area if it looks as though the interest in that area is there to stay. The key is that if you are publishing – or writing – in an established area, you have to be visibly better and to have a clear 'edge' in some respect.

Why is it so difficult to get your book published?

It's a commonly held belief that getting your book published is really hard work. Of course, the people who get their book accepted by the first person they send it to, immediately after sending it, don't believe that. But the rest of us do.

Well over 100,000 books are published each year in the UK alone. That's a staggering number. It suggests that it's actually not that difficult to get your book published at all. However this is only a tiny percentage of all the books that are submitted to publishers annually. Statistically, there's no doubt that it is hard to get published.

Some publishers will take on as many books as they come across each year that they really like and believe they can sell. Others, however, have 'title counts' – a set number of books they want to publish in any given year. Some have minimum financial targets for new books – so say they will only take a book on if they believe they can sell x thousand copies. So even if your book is good, and does appeal to the editor, it still doesn't always mean it will get picked up. Sometimes a publisher will have to choose between two books as they have only one 'slot' to fill. Other times a publisher will like your book but believe they can sell only 5,000 copies in the first year, when the minimum target is 10,000 for a book of that price.

And to get all the bad news out of the way at once, I'll have a final harbinger of doom moment and tell you that booksellers, and most publishers, generally believe there are too many books published each year.

> "I wish fewer people would write books and fewer publish them."
> *Andrew Franklin, MD, Profile*

It's probably fair to say that all our lives would be made easier if fewer books were published and of better quality. There wouldn't be so much competition for shelf space and good books would stand out better from the also rans, meaning it's better for the bookseller, the browser, the sales reps and the publisher.

But is it really that easy?

I'd like to meet the editor who never published a poor book. We all do it. Some more than others, but we all do it. It reminds me of many senior executives in publishing companies I've come across. Sooner or later, a new incumbent to the job (usually one without an editorial background) says something like 'I think we should publish fewer books and sell more of them.'

The whole commissioning team utters a weary sigh. 'No.... really? Why on earth didn't I think of that?' The truth is, you never really know for sure if any given book is going to take off or not. The uncertainty factor is part of the buzz for the editor, if not for the company. Publishing is not a science. I believe that as a publisher all you can do is to improve your ratio of hits to misses. That's partly down to knowing your market very well indeed, and largely down to having a finely honed gut instinct. But however good you are, you'll never get it right all the time.

> "One thing I came to realise is that publishing is so often a matter of luck."
> *Tom Maschler, quoted in the Daily Telegraph, from his autobiography* Publisher

Secondly (and this is where you come in, dear reader) I don't think fewer people should write books. I think as many people as want to should write books – it's fun, it's enjoyable, it stretches your brain and your vocabulary, it helps you work through thoughts and feelings, explore your creativity and keep records of things you've learned. I just think as writers, we need to think very hard about whether we really need to have a particular bit of writing published. In the traditional sense at least. Maybe we just need to consider more deeply, and with a bit more honesty, why we want something to be published.

Have you really looked at all the competition? Are you truly convinced the book will make your readers happier, better entertained, more successful? Does it really make a contribution to the world? It may be that your idea doesn't need to be published in the traditional sense – perhaps you'd be better served writing it as a blog on the web. Or making it available as an e-book that you can self publish. Or maybe you can publish it yourself and just have 200 copies for your own purposes. Chapter 3 will help you work through your reasons for wanting to have the book published – and Chapter 10 covers self publishing as an alternative approach to the traditional publishing route.

Finally, there's the sticky issue of what is a good book anyway? Who decides if there are enough books on keeping cats or gardening? Or enough sci-fi novels? Ultimately the number of books in any area is controlled by the number of people who are willing to buy them. It's that complex, and that simple. If a publisher is publishing too many books that don't sell, they won't survive as a business. If they can make enough money out of most of their books, then they will survive. Vive la choice?

What makes a good book?

If only there were an easy answer to this one. It's subjective – which is why you should never, ever be put off by a rejection from a single editor or agent or publisher. Here are some options, any of which could define a good book:

1. A book that sells well.
2. A book that gives pleasure to those who read it.
3. A book that wins literary or academic prizes.
4. A book that tells you what you need to know.
5. A book that changes the lives of those who read it.

Which of these will apply to your book idea? Honestly?

I do believe it is the responsibility of every publisher and more specifically every editor to be as rigorous as they possibly can in deciding what to publish. The more picky a publisher gets about what they publish, the more likely they are not to be adding to the also rans, but to be making a valuable contribution to the bookshelves of the world. In that respect, I agree with those who say there's a problem with overpublishing.

If publishers are to be more rigorous, then of course that makes your job as a would-be published author that little bit more challenging. But it probably is for the greater good. What it means for you is that (a) you need to think long and hard about whether you really want to do this and be very honest with yourself as to whether you can write well enough, (b) you need to consider seriously whether your book really needs/deserves to be published, and (c) if you decide yes, it does, you need to be very good indeed at convincing a publisher to agree with you. Let's do it.

2 How publishers and authors make money

An insider's guide to the financial side of publishing

If your book is to be published, a publisher has to believe they can profit from it, so it makes sense to look quickly at how the financial side of publishing works. In doing so we can look at how you as an author make money out of it too. (Maybe not as much as you expected.)

Publishing is an enormously complex business. However, the financial side – how the publisher and author actually make money – is one of the few relatively simple aspects.

Unless the publisher sells the book directly to the final customer (the reader) themselves, it receives nowhere near the cover price, or the recommended retail price, for the book. The booksellers take a big chunk – from about 35% up to 70% or more, depending on the type of book, the size of the market and the bookseller in question. The more copies of a book the bookseller takes, the greater the discount they can negotiate. Supermarkets therefore don't take many titles, but for those they take they can ask for an extraordinarily large discount. There has been a definite recent trend towards retailers demanding ever larger discounts which is hurting publishers. Sometimes the extra discount is passed on to the reader, thus stimulating book sales, but sometimes it isn't.

On top of this, the retailers are now increasingly asking publishers to pay for in-store marketing associated with promotions or placements (such as '3 for 2' offers or Book of the Month slots), as well as giving extra discount. There's no doubt this is making publishing more difficult. At the best of times it's a low margin business, but this is definitely making it harder to keep profit margins at a viable level.

As if this weren't tough enough, unless the publisher is big enough to have its own sales and distribution operation, it will also have to pay a third party to handle the sales and distribution – this could be up to an additional 25% of the cover price gone.

Let's take a worked example to illustrate this.

The cover price of our selected book is, say, £10. An average of 50% might be going to the bookseller, leaving the publisher with £5. If the publisher uses third party sales and distribution, then that's another 20% of the cover price gone, taking the £5 down to £3. The author gets say 50p in royalty. The cost of the paper and printing might be say £1 per copy, and there will be a proportion of other 'direct' costs to go against each copy, for example copyediting, jacket design, picture fees, permissions, typesetting etc (basically anything where external suppliers are used). When these costs have been deducted, the publisher will be left with somewhere between £1 and £3.50. From this, the publisher has to pay all indirect costs (all overheads for running the business, plus a share of marketing and publicity costs, etc). What's left is profit.

A low margin business indeed. It's also a very high risk business.

There is no guarantee that any one book will sell. At the decision making meeting where books are discussed, figures are run according to how many copies the publisher thinks they can sell at what price but of course for new books, especially those from new authors, it's really nothing better than educated guesswork.

For every bestseller a publisher has produced, there will be at least a couple of also rans and the odd massive disappointment. To be successful, what the publisher must do is keep their ratio of big sellers at a certain level. A publisher can afford so many disappointments, but not too many. The more you look at the risk and the uncertainty and the low margins, the more you wonder why anybody would start a publishing business. It also explains why there tends to be a high level of mergers and acquisitions in the publishing industry.

The reason I explain all this is that the better you understand the industry you are trying to sell a product to, the more likely you are to succeed. If you are the author of a literary work, I expect you'll be grimacing furiously now at having your carefully crafted piece of literary art described as a 'product' but, however you look at it, that's what it is. Sorry. The more you can convince a publisher that your book is going to be one of those big sellers (or big profit makers – if it can be a high priced book you don't necessarily need to sell huge numbers) the more likely you are to get taken on.

> "Losers set out to sell what they know they can make; winners set out to make what they know they can sell."
> *Sir Antony Jay, co-author of* Yes, Minister

Frontlist and backlist

Recent and forthcoming books are known as a publisher's frontlist and everything else is known as the backlist. Some publishers are very frontlist driven, by which we mean that sales from that year's new titles are absolutely vital to the success of the company. Other publishers are very backlist driven, which means that they have published a lot of very successful books in the past that keep on selling, and effectively underwrite the new titles. The more frontlist driven a publisher is, the more risky it is for them. There's a great deal of security to be had from a big solid backlist. As an author, if you get a big hit when your book publishes, it's fantastic to bask in the glow; but if it's longer term income you want, then producing a book that will backlist is a very good strategy. It generally means something that doesn't date, that isn't attached to a particular fad, and that stands a good chance of turning into a classic.

Illustrated publishing

The most difficult area of publishing in which to make a good profit has to be highly illustrated non-fiction – whether it's a glossy gardening book, a book about dinosaurs or yoga or pilates, an illustrated child's dictionary or a photographic guide to the Himalayas. The upfront investment costs are considerable: the books are usually designed page by page, there are picture fees and picture researchers to pay for, and that's not to mention the mandatory 4-colour printing costs. For this reason, highly illustrated publishing is normally driven by the ability to sell co-editions.

What this means is that before a glossy illustrated book is given the go ahead by the publisher, they will try and pre-sell the rights to the book in at least four or five territories/languages around the world. The foreign language publishers (known as co-edition publishers) buy the files of the pages, as laid out complete with pictures, and drop in their own translated text in place of the English. It's cheaper for the co-edition publisher than producing a book from scratch, and the income from the co-editions makes the book viable for the UK publisher.

> "The whole process is geared to the international readership."
> *Ian Jackson, Eddison Sadd, highly illustrated book packager*

Packagers are so called because they sell a complete package at a fixed price to foreign language co-edition publishers worldwide. The fixed price, for a set number of copies, includes an author royalty if applicable.

The effect of getting it wrong in illustrated publishing can be absolutely catastrophic for the company.

Case in point

Highly acclaimed publisher Dorling Kindersley was badly hit when it spectacularly misjudged the likely sales of an illustrated guide to *Star Wars Episode I* in 1999. By the end of the year, just three million of the 13 million copies printed had been sold. The company suffered massive financial losses for the year and was sold not long afterwards.

All this has implications for the would-be writer of illustrated non-fiction: high investment costs mean that 'author costs' will always be very acutely scrutinised, as margins are tight. If the idea for the book comes from the publisher or packager, you may well be offered a flat fee for writing the text rather than advance and royalty. It's likely not to be a huge amount, say maybe £4,000 for the average illustrated book. And on a flat fee basis, that's all you would get (see below).

Highly illustrated publishers and packagers spend a lot of time generating ideas for books themselves. There are real opportunities here for authors if you are willing to do proper research into the company and what it publishes and think hard about the international market and how well a book will co-edition. Generally, to be viable, the book concept will have to work in at least four countries outside the UK. Gift books are also high on the agenda of illustrated publishers. They sometimes produce books to sell directly to gift market retailers. Again, if you are serious about writing for this market, do lots of research and think it all through from the publisher's perspective. If you can generate commercially viable good ideas, you will be snapped up as an author.

Assessing the business risk

The decision as to whether to take on a particular book for publication is a complex one. The key factors include: how much the editor likes the book, how persuasive they are in selling it to their colleagues, how risky the publishing committee see it as being (especially the sales and marketing team) and the strategies of the publishing company.

The author advance is clearly part of the investment risk in a book by a publisher. Generally, a publisher calculates an advance on what it might reasonably expect to pay out in royalties in the book's first year. However, as the publisher has no way of knowing if the book will fly or crash and burn, this is largely guesswork. It probably goes without saying that most publishers try to reduce the amount that they pay out in advances, simply because it reduces their exposure to risk. They are very happy to pay out to the author in royalties as and when the book really takes off, but don't want to be paying out on the possibility that the book might earn that much.

However not all publishers see the advance in this light. Some, especially in fiction, see the advance as the cost of 'buying' the author. "The fact is, we are in a competitive marketplace – and the market determines the price of the author." said Malcolm Edwards of Orion Group in 2005. "In some ways, it's a mistake to think of the advance as something that's got to be earned by royalties. The advance to the author is the cost of having that author's book. What matters in the end is whether it yields sufficient profit." The more famous and bestselling you are, the more likely this is to apply to you. In other words, a publisher can still make a profit if the advance doesn't 'earn out' (ie if the royalties earned from copies sold never equals the amount already paid as an advance). For some publishers, they might not always expect the advance to earn out, but it's wise to assume that most publishers will want and expect it to.

> "Young editors are being taught to be risk-averse... They are going for the obvious choices or, tellingly, the novels which are in need of very little editorial work. Novels that merely show promise do not get sold – novels that are brilliant and in need of

> almost no attention do. All too often, it isn't the editor who calls the shots, but the dark forces of sales and marketing."
> *Simon Trewin, literary agent at PFD, in the* Independent on Sunday

Different publishers have different attitudes to risk, and view different books as risky. Sometimes an editor can get into a raging battle with sales and marketing colleagues because the editor wants to publish a particular book, but the sales and marketing team don't share the editor's sales expectations for the book. It's agony for the editor, because of course sales expectations are just that, expectations. You can't prove you are right in advance. Generally the better the track record of the editor, the more likely they are to be supported if they back a project, but there's always the exception. There are two reasons why it is important to understand this. Firstly, the more you can help the editor build a case for why your book will be successful, the better the chances of the editor convincing sales and marketing colleagues. Secondly, if the editor comes back and says your book has been rejected at the publishing meeting, it's probably down to a disagreement over how well it will sell. And another publisher might feel differently.

Case in point

An author of a book on starting a business received a conditional offer from a publisher. They would publish the book if the author secured an advance bulk sale to a bank. He had mentioned this was a possibility.

Another publisher, however, liked the book so much that they were happy to make the offer without the bulk sale. The book has been a roaring success – and the bulk sale happily came in too which made it doubly good.

How you earn money from having your book published

There are two main ways an author can be paid by a publisher for writing a book:

1 A flat fee

The author receives a one-off payment for what they write or have written, and in return they sign over copyright for that piece of work to the publisher. In effect the publisher has bought a piece of writing from you. This is most common in illustrated non-fiction books (sport, gardening, illustrated guides etc), especially if the publisher had the idea and approached the author to write it. Sometimes it is even calculated on a price per thousand words (maybe around £100-120 per thousand words).

The advantage of a flat fee is that you know exactly how much you will earn, and that even if the book doesn't do well, you will have received your money. The disadvantage is that even if the book goes on to sell tens or hundreds of thousands, you don't get a penny more.

2 An advance and a royalty

This is the more common payment arrangement. The royalty is the amount of money you receive per book sold. The royalty is a percentage of either the recommended retail price (the price printed on the book cover), or a percentage of the 'net receipts' (normally calculated as the cover price of the book, minus whatever the bookseller takes as their cut). By 'the bookseller' we might mean just the actual bookstore itself, for larger publishers who sell direct, or we might mean the bookstore and the distributor.

Royalty on published price

This is the more common way of calculating royalty for fiction (and some non-fiction, depending on the type of publisher). It means that you get an agreed percentage of the cover price, irrespective of the size of discount given to the retailer.

The starting royalty for hardback books is usually 10% of published price, and for paperbacks 7.5% of published price.

So for example, if you get a royalty of 7.5% of published price, and the book retails at £6.99, you get 7.5% of £6.99 or 52p per copy. This is what you receive whether the book is sold at the full £6.99 or in a sale or at discounted price.

Royalty on net receipts

This is widespread for many non-fiction publishers, especially educational or academic publishers and illustrated publishers/packagers, but not exclusively. It means that you get a percentage of whatever amount the publisher gets for the book from the bookseller. So for example if the cover price of the book is £10 and the bookseller buys the book from the publisher at 50% discount, then the net receipt on which the royalty is calculated will be £5. The royalty rate for net receipts contracts should be higher than the royalty rate for published price contracts, so that the actual amount the author receives is roughly similar.

A typical starting royalty rate for a net receipts contract would be 10% of net receipts. So if the cover price is £6.99 and the bookseller gets 45% discount, the publisher would get £3.84 for the book and the author would get 10% of £3.84 which is 38p.

Two things to note here:

1 Some publishers use published price to calculate royalty for home sales (by which they mean sales in the UK, or wherever is 'home') and net receipts to calculate royalty for 'export' or overseas sales.

2 The figures I quote are just a guide, they aren't absolute – you may get less or you may get more. It's an indication of roughly what to expect.

Flat or escalating royalty

Whether you get a contract based on published price or net receipts, it is fairly common to get an escalating royalty so that the more copies of the book are sold, the higher the percentage of the royalty you get. So, for example, you might start off at 10% of net receipts, but when 10,000 copies have been sold, the royalty might increase to 12.5% and then when 20,000 copies have been sold, you might increase to 15% of net receipts.

Similarly on published price you might start on 7.5% of published price, but increase in steps to 10% after so many copies have been sold. You tend to have to sell more copies on a published price deal to go up to a higher royalty rate. Escalators on net receipts tend to rise more quickly.

Advance

The advance is the amount of money the publisher pays you up front, after the contract is signed but before your book is published. Be warned, it is an 'advance on royalties' which means that you are receiving a big chunk of your royalties up front, in advance of the books selling and the royalties being earned. If you get a big advance it could take a long time for the advance to 'earn out' (ie for the book to sell enough copies so that what you have earned per copy cancels out what you were paid up front). It may therefore be a long time before you get any more cash. You may indeed never see any more money than your advance.

In theory, under some publishing contracts, the publisher could ask for any part of the advance that has not earned out to be paid back, although in practice this is rare. Check your contract to see if the advance is non-returnable.

Advances are normally paid in two or three instalments. The first part is paid on signature of contract, then you may get a second part on delivery and acceptance of the manuscript and/or a second or third part on publication of the book.

The amount of advance varies across an immense spectrum, from nothing to a six figure sum. However, you can be sure that there are a lot more advances nearer the zero end than at the big bucks end of this spectrum.

You might be offered a combination of part flat fee and part advance and royalty.

We'll look at how important advances and royalties are to you in the next chapter, as part of the process of choosing a publisher, and then how to negotiate them with the publisher in Chapter 7.

What other income can an author expect?

Other income will include revenue from the sale of rights, mainly foreign language rights – all income from translation deals is split between author and publisher. The revenue generated this way can vary from nothing to a considerable amount. The issue of what rights you should give a publisher, and what proportion you might expect to receive of rights sold, is covered in depth in Chapter 7 which is all about contracts.

Case in point

Sometimes rights income really does count. I've known a number of practical books that for various reasons didn't sell terribly well in the home (UK) market but were a huge hit with foreign language publishers. If, as in these cases, a book doesn't sell very well in the UK but gets six or seven translation deals or more, the income from these rights deals can actually be greater than income from royalties of books sold in English.

One source of income that you need to take control of personally is Public Lending Rights (PLR). Under the PLR scheme, authors receive payments from government funds for the free borrowing of their books from UK public libraries. However, you as the author have to apply to register the book with the PLR office to receive anything. Every year a sample of libraries monitor which books they have lent out, and how many times, and these figures are used to calculate how much of the total lending rights pot of cash for all authors you will receive. Go to the PLR website at **www.plr.uk.com** for more information and to register, as soon as your book is published.

The Authors' Licensing and Collecting Society (ALCS) collects and distributes money to authors whose work has been broadcast, copied or recorded. It also collects money from lending and rental sources. Most of its income comes from licensed photocopying. The ALCS together with the Publishers' Licensing Society (PLS) have appointed the Copyright Licensing Authority (CLA) to act as the licensing agent. Basically, the CLA collects the money and divides it between the ALCS (who pay the author) and the PLS (who pay the publisher). It won't be a huge amount of money, but hey, it could be extra income. In order to receive any money, you have to join the ALCS (**www.alcs.co.uk**). Full membership carries a fee, but allows you access to a legal advisory service. Associate membership is free, but there is a handling charge deducted from any monies owed to you.

These are the direct sources of income – there may be other, indirect, sources of income such as serialisation rights, or fees for articles you may be asked to write as a result of getting your book published. Some authors may also generate revenue from speaking work as a result of getting published.

Case in point

One author tells of how she's been paid fees of up to £1,000 several times for feature articles she's written around the theme of her book. They obviously provided fabulous PR for the book, and the extra income is very welcome.

Don't assume you will get paid for feature articles however – some media are wise to the fact that you are getting great PR from them, and won't be so ready to part with cash in return.

For most authors, income isn't the only factor in their desire to get published (thankfully) – the reasons for wanting to get published, and how this should affect your choice of publisher, are explored in the next chapter.

3 Choosing the right publisher for you

How to find the most appropriate company to approach

It's possible you have already tried to get a publisher for your book. In this case you will be looking at the title of this chapter thinking, in a voice of quiet desperation, that any publisher would do never mind the right one. It's not just about being picky, however – knowing who you are approaching and why can increase your chances of success in getting published, and your happiness with what happens thereafter.

Simply put, if you choose the right kind of publisher for your needs and for your book, you are much more likely to have it accepted and be happy with the result. As in any kind of business, all publishing companies are different. They have different values, publish different combinations of book genres, and have different book selection criteria. Each will have a different publishing ethos, and place different weighting on sales, marketing and editorial support. The aim is to work out who will be your ideal partner – after all it is another kind of relationship.

Even if you have an agent (or are thinking about one, see the next chapter) it's a good idea to think about what it is you are looking for in a publisher. Even with an agent as matchmaker, the more you know about your ideal partner, the better your chances of winning them.

Golden rule

The first step to finding the right publisher is to think about why you want to have your book published.

Your reasons for wanting to get published

People want to get published for myriad reasons. It's definitely worth spending a bit of time thinking about why you want to have your book published, and what you want from it, as this should guide what kind of publisher you go for.

Here are some of the more common reasons for wanting to get your book published (in no particular order):

- Fame
- Money
- So that I can give up my job and become an author full time
- Literary acclaim
- Because I've written it
- To say something to the world/disseminate my message
- As a marketing tool for me/my company
- To raise my academic profile
- To see if it's any good
- Because my wife/husband/boyfriend/girlfriend/friend/relative/boss says I should
- So I can leave it behind – a kind of legacy

- To help people deal with/work through something
- Because I think it's quite good
- Because I'm an expert in something
- Because I don't want it to sit in a cupboard forever
- Because I don't want to have wasted a year of my life writing it for nothing
- Just to see something I wrote in print
- Because I've got the idea and I want to write it
- Because I can
- Because a publisher has asked me to

Most would-be authors have at least one and probably several of these reasons on their list. Now is the time to sit down and pick your top three reasons for wanting to have your book published and then to prioritise them.

Decide also how serious you are about this whole venture. Is it just a bit of fun? Are you just having a punt and seeing if it pays off? Or are you absolutely committed to getting published, and ideally having a career as a writer? Maybe somewhere in between. One very well published author says he thinks that "90% of writers play at it". They vaguely fancy the idea of being able to say that they are a writer, but they have no intention of investing proper effort into it and the commitment isn't there. Unless you are really very serious, have invested time and effort in getting this far, and are ready to invest much, much more, then your chances of getting published are pretty slim. Dedication, commitment and passion for writing, plus a willingness to really work at the craft are very important indeed.

Some words of caution

So far, I've been encouraging about you writing your book and getting it published – after all, that's what this book is about. However, it's only fair to provide a reality check too.

Here are three of the not-so-good reasons you might want to get published, with a few words about them:

1 Money/fame

Only a very, very small percentage of published authors make decent money from it. For the vast majority of writers, considering the time it takes to write a book and the return you get from it, you would be much better off doing something else. I'd really strongly advise against writing in the expectation of getting rich or famous. You might be one of the very lucky tiny minority, but you're more likely not to be. There's got to be another reason to want to be published.

2 Because I can

I would worry about this reason probably more than any other. A lot of people can write about a lot of things (sometimes well, sometimes not so well). But it's no good unless somebody wants to read it. Think about this.

3 Because my partner/parents/friends say I should

Friends and family tend to be nice about their loved ones and their abilities. They aren't terribly objective. 'That's very good, you should write a book!' is usually a loving comment, rather than a literal suggestion. First, think about whether you really want to do it and whether you really have the aptitude. Secondly think about whether anybody will want to read what you write – why would they pick your book up? Finally, try and get an impartial view of your idea and your ability before you go any further.

With those out of the way, go back to your major reasons for wanting to get published. Then sit down for a minute or two, close your eyes and imagine a year's time when your book is published. What does it look like? Where is it in the shop? What's happening around it? The clearer your picture, the more it will help you work out if you've considered where your book sits in the marketplace and if indeed there is a market for it. Like it or not, being able to think in marketing terms is part of your job as a writer. If you find it very difficult, ask a friend or colleague to help. It will also help you raise awareness of your needs and expectations, and these are important in finding the right publisher for you.

At this point you may have what publishers might refer to as 'unrealistic expectations'. If the book you are planning is about keeping chickens, then a 10 city book signing tour is pretty unrealistic, as is a six figure advance and a dump bin with 100 copies in every bookstore in the UK. We'll try to set reasonable expectations when we look at the specifics of a publishing deal, but for now it's just worth having a quick reality peck, I mean check.

So, now you are clear on why you want to have your book published, and this will give you some pointers on what you might need to look for in a publisher. S0 what now? A quick look at *The Writers' and Artists' Yearbook/The Writer's Handbook* will show just how many publishers there are to choose from. How do you know which ones would be the best for you and for your book?

Here's the essential guide on how to decide:

Find the right publishers for your subject

Go to a bookshop, search on amazon and find out who already publishes in the field of your book. What are the classics in the area? What are the new books? Can you tell what's selling well? And what isn't shifting? It's definitely worth asking the bookseller if a particular book is selling well – depending what kind of person you happen across (if they are a true bookseller or more of a shop assistant) they could be extremely useful. Get a really good sense of what's out there. Rankings of books on amazon.co.uk aren't an absolute indicator, and some of the 'bestseller lists' are a bit unreliable as they rely on books being properly categorised (which isn't always the case) but it gives you a good idea.

Make lots of notes on the competition for your book, if it's that kind of book – you'll need that later. If your book isn't the kind that has competition per se then have a look around and think what your target reader might be picking up because your book isn't there. For example, if your book is a populist history of time and how we've measured it through the ages, then what other intelligent populist science or history books are browsers going for?

Have a look to see what books really attract you, both in your area and in other parts of the shop. What kinds of book can you see that you'd like your book to be like? What size are they, what kind of cover do they have? And most importantly, who publishes them?

Look at other books by the same publisher. Are they all similar? Can you tell anything about the 'personality' of the publisher (known also as the 'brand values' in business speak)? Does it fit with yours? Just because two publishers produce books for the same market doesn't mean they are at all similar – every children's book publisher for example has a different personality, a different look and tone and style. Highlight those publishers who appeal to you and have the best fit with the style and content of your book.

Think categories

Within fiction, publishers (and booksellers) usually divide books up into these core categories:

- Historical
- Romance
- Crime/mystery
- Sci-fi/fantasy/horror
- Thrillers
- Westerns
- War
- Action/adventure

Outside these categories, there is a big wide ranging group known as 'general fiction', and a smaller group that is loosely termed 'literary fiction'. The latter as a term is more used by publishers and agents than readers.

It pays to think about whether your book fits into any of these categories, as this might affect your choice of publisher. The same is true for non-fiction of course: is it a business book or popular psychology or mind/body/spirit? If you're not sure, think about where you would expect people to look for the book in a bookstore.

Beware the book that you think could sit in several places… The chances of a new book being 'double stocked' – shelved in more than one area of a bookstore – are slim indeed. Choose where you think it fits best, and that will affect your choice of publisher.

Bear in mind also, if you have ideas for more than one book, in more than one genre, that you might want to place both books with the same publisher. In which case, does a particular publisher cover all the subjects that interest you?

Right subject, right publisher

You would be truly amazed how many people send book proposals to publishers who are completely inappropriate. A book on shamans sent to a medical textbook publisher. A novel synopsis sent to a popular psychology publisher. A children's book posted to a business publisher. I promise you I have seen all the above. It's such a waste of time and money, and it shows that the author just hasn't done their research at all. This won't be you of course.

> **Insider's view**
>
> The book proposal arrives on my desk. Immediately it's obvious that the sender hasn't even bothered to see what I publish – it's completely the wrong subject or completely the wrong level. Although I know editors who do publish in this area, there's nothing in the covering note that gives me the inclination to send it on to them, so it goes straight in the bin.

The idea here is to identify a shortlist of publishers who publish in the right area, or conceivably might do. (A publisher who does general illustrated non-fiction including books on legendary military leaders and famous explorers for example might well accept an illustrated book on religious leaders.) When you've got a shortlist, have a look at what each one has published already and quickly note what the key titles are and what you think of them.

If a publisher already has a book that's very close to the one you are thinking of, it might mean that there's little point approaching that company. For example, a publisher is unlikely to want two books on, say, adopting a greyhound, or the early years of Oscar Wilde. However, if the subject area is similar but the books have a different angle or are aimed at a different level, this could be a good choice of company to approach. For example, if a publisher has done a book on starting a business, they may well be interested in another if it's starting a business with no cash or for people with no business experience.

Generally, publishers like clusters of books as it means they can market and promote them together, and run promotions around themes. Remember that books are low ticket items and therefore anything that can spread marketing spend further is good for a publisher.

It also means you know the publisher is interested in the area your book falls into. If they have recently published a historical novel, chances are they might be interested in another.

The subject shortlist

Once you've drawn up a shortlist of publisher prospects, it's a good idea to check out what you can find out from them from other sources: their websites, other websites, *The Bookseller* (a weekly magazine for the book trade), *Publishing News*, their authors and so on. At this point you are looking for anything about their philosophy, their standing in the marketplace, their values, anything that might affect their fit with you and your book – and their ability to do a great job for you.

Big or small?

One of the major differences between publishers will be size. But does it matter? The publishing sector is dominated by a small number of huge publishers. It's not always apparent as each publisher may use up to five or six 'imprints' or brand names. For example Random House publishes under imprints including Vintage, Vermillion, Arrow and so on. Even more confusing is the fact that one parent organisation might own more than one publishing company – Pearson plc owns Penguin and Dorling Kindersley as well as the huge Pearson Education group for example. For a list of who owns what, see *The Writers' and Artists' Yearbook/The Writer's Handbook.*

However, there are also literally hundreds of small publishers, any of whom could be absolutely perfect for your book.

One of the decisions you need to make is whether you have any preference for a large or small company. There are some clear pros and cons for each, as your choice will depend on what it is that's important to you, what you want to publish and what you want out of it. Here's a quick summary of the main points to consider:

Small Publisher

The main pros are:

1 **Attention** A small publisher is more likely to focus really hard on each title – you won't just be a small cog in a big machine. If the publisher is publishing just six titles a year you should get much more attention than you would anywhere else – this could mean a much better PR and marketing effort (this is not universally true, so pick your small publisher carefully). You're a big part of their business and it should show.

2 **Flexible, innovative, responsive** If just one or two people run the company, you're more likely to get a quick decision, and ideas are likely to be put into action quickly. They can usually react faster to market trends and will be willing to capitalise on opportunities that big publishers might see as too small. The innovative approach often runs through the company and includes the sales effort – if you're small you often try and build a personal relationship with the retailers and other outlets – it can work amazingly well.

And the main cons:

1 **Sales and distribution** It's unlikely to be as slick as a big house – they will probably use a third party sales and distribution service. Ask about their sales set up. If a bigger publisher distributes them, their books are likely to be last out of the rep's book bag. As a general rule, you aren't likely to see as many copies of their books in as many stores. There are exceptions however. If the small publisher is punching above their weight by being smart and personal with retailers, they can do very well. I know of at

least two small publishers who get personal audiences with the top buyers in top chains, despite the common belief that small publishers don't get a look in. Pick your small publisher with care.

2 **The financial deal** You're unlikely to get a big advance, if any. By their nature, small publishers don't have the resources to offer six figure sums.

Big publisher

The main pros here are:

1 **Size and strength**

Increasingly booksellers are reducing the number of sales reps they see and generally the biggest are seen most often. If a publisher is large, they can push booksellers hard for promotions and on numbers of copies a store takes, as the bookseller does need them to supply the bestsellers on which the bookseller makes the guaranteed money. Additionally, a large publisher will almost certainly have its own sales force instead of using a third party or distributor. Perceived wisdom is that publisher owned sales forces do a better job as a rule. All other things being equal, you are likely to sell many more copies through bookstores with a big publisher as opposed to a small one.

2 **Big wallets**

Not always (see the section on Money below) but on average the cash reserves are healthier and you're likely to earn more.

3 **Prestige**

It can be good to be published by a company people have heard of.

And the main cons:

1 Small cog, big wheel

You won't be as important to a big publisher as you are to a small one. Big publishers are sometimes accused of watching which books take off and then backing them, while leaving others to sink or swim. Darwinian publishing I guess you could call it.

2 Bureaucracy

There are systems and processes in big publishers. Forms have to be filled in and signed and there are protocols and practices. It can take longer for things to happen and there is more to get in the way. The right hand may not know what the left hand is doing.

Of course, even if you choose a small publisher, you might end up being part of a big one. It is very common for a small publisher to start and then be swallowed up by a bigger group.

Publishers are usually small for one of three reasons:

1 They have started up relatively recently and are still growing.
2 They want to remain small (and therefore retain control).
3 They serve a niche market.

When looking at your options among small publishers, it's worth thinking about which of the three might apply to each, and whether that suits you. For example, if a publisher is clearly in a growth phase, it's quite possible they may decide to sell up to a bigger publisher before too long – your book would then end up with a big house but possibly given very little attention. However, you could also look at it as a back door way to being published by a big house.

Specialist or general publisher?

There is a handful of publishing houses who publish in both fiction and non-fiction, albeit usually under different imprints, and in a vast range of subject areas. Examples include Penguin, Random House, Harper Collins, Transworld and (the only independent in this group) Faber and Faber.

At the opposite extreme are the very specialised, usually smaller, publishers who only do books in one very specialised area (for example, medicine or religion).

Between these are the other publishers, large and small, who concentrate on a few core areas that are related to each other, such as illustrated non-fiction in cookery, gardening, and lifestyle. Or historical and romantic novels only.

Publishers in these different groups do behave differently so this is worth bearing in mind. For example, the generalist is most likely to pay royalties on published price for all books, fiction or non-fiction, and may be accustomed to larger advances. The more specialised publishers, however, are much more likely to be able to know their markets inside out, and this should make them better positioned to help you craft your idea to be as good as it can possibly be, and to reach the market more specifically.

Size of market

The size of market might have an immediate bearing on who will consider your book: many publishers, especially larger ones, will only take on books that they can sell a certain number of copies of, as they don't want a huge list of books that sell a few hundred copies a year. If only 2,000 people adopt an ex-racing greyhound each year in the UK, then at best you will be looking at a few hundred copies a year, so you might be better off looking at a small specialist animal book publisher than one of the huge trade publishing houses. Those kinds of numbers aren't going to be enough to excite them.

Money

If your primary aim is to make money out of having your book published, then you need to be clear that the chances of making big money are slim. As discussed in Chapter 2, the returns might not be so great, and there are almost always quicker, easier and more sure-fire ways of making money. I'd be very nervous if anybody told me that they were giving up a day job to be a full time writer without a contract for several books. And even then I'd probably have a reserve plan. You've seen from the royalty examples on pp.34-35 that you have to sell a lot of books at 50p a copy royalty to make a decent living.

Putting the warning aside, if money is an important factor to you, then this will affect your choice of publisher. There are two types of money to consider – the up front and the longer term. As seen on p.33 you are most likely to be paid with an advance and royalty, but could be offered a flat fee.

More up front

You might decide that the most important thing for you is to get as much cash up front as you can, and you don't care what happens thereafter. In this case, your best bet is to choose a publisher that offers the largest possible advance. Publishers vary widely on the size of advance they offer. Some publishers will fight and win bidding wars at all costs; others simply won't compete on advances and view the advance as simply to cover the author's costs in getting the manuscript completed.

Clearly the size of advance you can negotiate depends on the kind of book you are writing. You might get anywhere between nothing and a six figure sum, with something near the former being far more likely than something close to the latter. For most non-fiction books something between £1,000 and £10,000 should give you an idea. The average is probably in the lower half of that range.

So how do you find out what kind of advance you might expect from a particular publisher? If you have an agent they should be able to advise on who would be best for the biggest advance. The Society of Authors if you are a member can give you a ballpark figure for the kind of book you are writing. If you are working solo, then here are some rough guidelines to choosing a publisher on the basis of highest advance:

1. Small publishers don't tend to pay as big an advance as big publishers do. For bigger advances, think bigger publishers.
2. However, small but fast growing publishers eager to make a name for themselves quickly may dig deep to sign the right book – look out for them.
3. Don't be afraid to ask a publisher roughly what size of advance they would offer if they did make you an offer. They might give you an indicator.

4 The easiest way to get a big advance is to have more than one publisher interested, so you might well think about multiple submissions (see p.128). Use the fact that you have another publisher interested to press for an early indicator of what the financial package might look like. Be honest and tell a publisher if you've a better offer elsewhere and ask if they can better it. There's only one vital rule though – don't bluff. They may well find out and you could end up with no publisher.

But does size matter? There are those who believe that the more a publisher pays in the way of an advance, the more effort they will put into selling a book, as they need to recoup the money paid out. And thus you should go for as much advance as you can possibly get. This is certainly true for some publishers but it's equally certainly not true for others. In most companies the sales and marketing staff will have no idea how much advance was paid out for a particular book and therefore it's not possible that this would influence how much effort they put in. The effort is proportional to how convinced they are that they can sell the book, and how much the booksellers are interested in buying it.

Some publishing companies calculate the advance they are willing to offer on the basis of what they might reasonably expect to sell in the first year and the royalty that would earn for the author. They will then give this up front.

Going back to the point about publishing being high risk, if you are after a big advance, you increase the risk to the publisher. Generally, anything you can do to reduce the risk increases the chances of you getting offers from more companies. Remember that advance is just that – an advance on what you would be getting in any case. Do you really need as much of it up front as possible? The longer term view is worth considering – it's what I would be interested in as an author.

There are some who believe that there should be a health warning on big advances for first time authors. Hari Kunzru has talked about how an author he knows received a huge advance, went off the rails and then found their book didn't sell, at which point nobody wanted to touch him. He was determined that the same shouldn't happen to him, and actually sought to tone down that first advance: "I didn't want them to pay a lot. I wanted them to pay enough."

Is a large advance an indicator of your likely success? I wouldn't take it as a very reliable indicator – legendary stories abound in publishing about the paltry sums paid for what became huge sellers. JK Rowling's first advance is rumoured to have been no more than £10,000. Trinny and Susannah are said to have got about £2,000 for the book *What Not To Wear* that went on to sell tens of thousands of copies as a Christmas 'must have' in 2003. The advance for *Men are from Mars, Women are from Venus* was apparently £3,000. And from personal experience, my biggest selling book with over 100,000 copies sold of the UK edition alone, had an advance of just £4,000.

The longer term strategy

The amount of money you'll receive from your book in the longer term depends on two factors: how many copies are sold and your royalty rate. If you are confident your book will sell well, then it makes sense that you concentrate on getting the best deal you can on your royalty rate. It's always a wise author in my view who is more concerned about the royalty rate than about the advance – it says two things: firstly that they are smart and understand how to maximise their revenue and secondly, that they have confidence in their book. If the author is interested in their income beyond the advance it gives me added confidence in the book's potential too.

It pays to be interested in royalty rates.

When choosing a publisher, you need to look for the one that offers you the best starting royalty rate, and the best escalator. That is, deals where the royalty rate increases at certain sales hurdles. Usually this is a good point for negotiation. So when investigating publishers, it's worth finding out if they are more or less generous than average on royalty rates. Unfortunately this is something you can't necessarily predict, as it doesn't bear correlation to the size of the publisher or any other particular factor. Generally, most publishers will negotiate on this point, so when choosing a publisher, just be ready to ask the question about royalty rates as soon as they show interest in the book.

What you then need to balance out is how many copies a publisher is likely to sell, versus what you will be paid per copy. This is where the size of company might come in. If longer term money is the big driving factor for you, then you would probably be better off looking for a bigger company and the best royalty rate you can get, as generally larger publishers find it easier to get books on shelves in quantity than smaller publishers.

What can they do for you?

Many authors are more interested in what having their book published can do for their career more generally, as opposed to the revenue just from the book itself. Having a book published can open lots of doors for a person. It acts as the best kind of business card, and establishes you immediately as an expert on whatever it is you've written about (and sometimes more broadly). It can be useful in pitching for work on TV. It can attract business to you.

This applies mostly to non-fiction, but it can apply to fiction too. I know of authors who just wanted to be able to say, 'look, I've had my novel published'.

If the profile that results from your book is important to you then here are some things very worth considering when looking for a publisher.

1 What is the PR record of the publisher? How many press articles have you seen for books from this publisher? What PR support might they provide? Don't assume that bigger publishers will have better PR. White Ladder Press (the small publisher of this book) have achieved some of the best PR I have ever seen, publicity that would put a lot of the big publishing houses to shame. Ideally you want a publisher either with a publicist in house or that will guarantee you a freelance publicist.

   This might be the biggest single factor if you are interested in the profile of having your book published.

2 How flexible is the marketing set-up at the publisher? Will they provide flyers if you are going to an event and have the opportunity to distribute some? Do they attend meetings where they can promote your book to a network you'd like to influence?

3 Author networks – does the publisher publish other authors whose networks could be useful to you? Are they proactive about introducing authors to each other?

4 Imprint – brand strength. Does the publisher's brand add anything to the profile of you or your book? For example, if your book on business planning was published with the FT brand, would that help? Or would it be helpful to have your book on spirituality published under the same roof as Deepak Choprah's books?

5 Stand alone or series? If your book looking unique and standing alone is important to you, steer away from series publishers. Series publishing can be great for getting shelf space as the range of books tends to be stocked together, but you are unlikely to get good PR profile out of it.

I just want it in print

If this is the case, then apply to as broad a cross-section of publishers as you can. If you don't mind where it goes, then give it the best chance of going somewhere. Self publishing is also an option if just having the book published as a business card is important to you. If you aren't worried about the books being in shops, and you just want them to be able to give away, this is a strong option (see Chapter 10).

I want to be a full time writer

If you want to get your book published as a prelude to a career in writing, there is a dilemma to consider when choosing a publisher to approach. In many ways, it would make a lot of sense to use your first book proposal to build a relationship with as many publishers as possible. The more publishers you know, the more likely they are to offer books to you as well as looking at your ideas.

Insider's view

Publishers offering books to authors? Yes – this does happen! Publishers do have ideas for books and they do approach authors to write them. See page 62 for how to improve your chances of getting asked.

Additionally, publishers sometimes actively encourage authors they know and like to sit and think up some new ideas to send in to them. I know one author who has just had a publisher ask her to send in ideas for 10 more books. (I realise it may be galling to learn that while you are desperately labouring away trying to get somebody even to look at your proposal, other people are being asked to come up with ideas, even if they don't have any. Sorry.)

However, tread carefully if there are particular publishers you like, and who you'd like to write for. In this case then it's a good idea to try and use the proposal to build as good a relationship as possible with that one publisher. If you build a trusting relationship with a publisher and they know you won't run off to the next bidder, they should go out of their way to support you. Generally if publishers don't trust you, or think you might play them off against another publisher, the feeling of goodwill isn't going to be so strong.

If you are serious about being a full time writer, it might be an idea to get an agent (see Chapter 4) as a good agent should play a part in bringing books to you as well as helping you sell yours to the right publishers.

Other ways to build your writing into a full time occupation could include becoming a ghostwriter, where you write a book for somebody, usually in their voice.

Another tactic, worth considering if you are very serious about writing full time, is to enrol on a good writing course. Another insider tells me that there are fiction editors who keep close tabs on the people accepted on the top writing courses. As learning your craft is obviously something you will be doing anyway, you might want to consider applying for one of the best courses in order to boost your chances of getting noticed. Competition for places is fierce so getting accepted on the course won't be a doddle.

How to get publishers to offer a book to you

In non-fiction, it's reasonably common for the publisher to have the idea and then go and look for the author to write it. But what can you do to increase your chances of them asking you?

1 Raise your profile. You have to make it easy for publishers to find you. Write articles or columns, in print or online. It doesn't matter how small the circulation is or how new the website – start somewhere and keep trying. Put yourself forward to radio stations as a possible commentator on areas in which you have expertise.

2 Network like crazy. The more people you meet, the more likely it is that when a publisher is looking for potential authors for a book on your subject (whether it's cats, children, personal coaching or nutrition) it's you that people think of first.

3 Teach your subject if you can. Especially for non-fiction that requires somebody with expertise, if you're teaching it you are at an advantage.

4 Try and find opportunities to speak to groups small or large on your subject. This has the effect of both raising profile and making you the first person others think of.

5 Get a website. The internet is the no.1 research tool for publishers now. Most of us don't know where we'd be without it. If a publisher knows what subject they want to publish on, they are quite likely to put that term into a search engine and see what comes up. Make sure your name does.

6 Get a good agent. Good agents may be asked by publishers if they know anybody who can write on a subject.

7 If there are a couple of books already around on a subject you know you can write well on, choose a competitor publisher and ask them if they've ever considered adding a book on x to their list as you notice it's something they don't have and you believe you can write a better one than the competitor's. For example, if you are an aromatherapist, you might look at all the introductory level guides to aromatherapy. If there's a publisher who does have books in the natural health area but doesn't have an introductory guide to aromatherapy, it's well worth asking them if they've considered one.

The personal touch

Some authors do pick their publishing house because of a particular editor they want to work with. I think that's a great reason, but then as an editor I'm clearly biased. Your editor is however the person with whom you have the strongest relationship. This is the person you are relying on to understand you and your book, to help you improve what you've written, to promote it internally and to the world.

How to find an individual editor who will be right for you

1 If there's a book you particularly admire, have a look in the acknowledgements. Does it list the editor's name and what they did for the author? If that's what you want, then it makes complete sense to pick the publisher so you can have that editor too.

2 If you can, talk to people who have published with different companies – ask them how they got on with their editor (and the marketing team and other key players).

3 Check your gut feeling about the editors you have contact with. Do you like the sound of them? Are they enthusiastic (and by this I don't mean are they crawling all over you, I mean can you sense genuine optimism about you and your book)? Is the advice they are giving constructive? Do you feel the person would be good to work with? If you are lucky enough to have the choice of more than one publisher, I believe that gut feeling about who you'd like to work with is as good a basis to choose as any.

So, now you've got your shortlist, you know who you want to approach – but do you need an agent?

4 Agents

How to decide if you need one, finding a good one and the real truth about publishers and agents

The term agent is usually short for literary agent or authors' agent. As this suggests, the agent's job is to represent you, the author. The idea is that once an agent has accepted you as a client, they will make sure your book submissions get on the desks of the right commissioning editors, get read and that you get the best possible deal. All without you having to lift a finger. In return for which they take between 10 and 20% of what you earn from the publishing deal.

A good agent is a priceless asset. They provide advice on your proposal, helping craft a submission to make it as attractive as possible, they make sure your submission gets read by those who possibly wouldn't look at it otherwise, they are respected by the publisher, they are extremely good at playing off publishers against each other thus pushing up the value of your work, they take negotiations to an art form, and are razor sharp at spotting contractual clauses that might go against you and having them removed or altered. They truly represent you and will add so much value to you that they more than compensate for their cut.

A bad agent, however, could cost you dearly. They add little or no value to your idea and publishers actually groan when a submission arrives with their name on the covering letter, simply because the publisher can't bear to think of dealing with them. And what's worse, they take 10% or more of all your earnings, money you could have pocketed because the publisher would have looked at your submission anyway, and given you exactly the same terms as the agent might get.

Golden rule

A bad agent is much worse than no agent at all. If you are going to have an agent it's very, very important to get a good one.

However, before we look at finding the right agent for you, the first step is to decide whether you need one or not.

How to decide if you need an agent – or if you'd be better going it alone

There are publishers who won't consider anything that doesn't come via an agent. If you want to be considered by them, you have no choice. It is generally agreed that though not essential to getting published, having an agent will boost your chances in fiction and some general non-fiction.

So, surely much better to have an agent and therefore make sure you get considered by everybody? Well, not necessarily. You might be giving away 10% or more of your future earnings when you didn't have to, in some cases. And then there's the fact that there are non-fiction editors who can't stand some agents and avoid them like the plague.

There are types of publishing where you do have the option of going it alone, and it might suit you to do so. For example, the more specialist your subject, the less likely you are to need an agent. Highly illustrated book ideas will often be considered without an agent. Smaller publishers also tend to be more open to submissions from authors, even in fiction. Poetry publishers tend to be open to direct submissions, if you have a good track record of getting published in magazines first.

Finding a good agent can also be difficult. There are far more would-be fiction authors than there are good agents, and the best ones are very much in demand. Some agents do actually claim to have 'full books' and say that they can properly represent only so many authors at any one time and so have to have a limit. Sounds fair enough, but it's hard to believe they would actually turn down a work of staggering genius if it were offered to them. Other good agents say that though they are always at or near client capacity, they would never turn down a brilliant new author, however many people they are representing. There's always time to be squeezed in somewhere they say.

The biggest publishers, again especially fiction, can get dozens of submissions a day. Just to cope they tend to give preference to agents' submissions in the hope that the agents will have weeded out the bad submissions. However, it is worth knowing that although many of the bigger publishers especially say 'no unsolicited submissions' (ie proposals from agents only, unpublished authors need not apply), some non-fiction editors are mindful of the huge bestsellers that have been rejected and may get editorial assistants, interns or readers to go through the 'slush pile' – the insider term for unsolicited submissions – and read some.

Insider's view

One non-fiction editor told me that though the official policy of his company was that unsolicited submissions were not accepted, any that did come in were piled up and that editorial assistants did scan through them if and when they had time. Occasionally the editorial assistants would bring him a submission that they thought might have merit; however, he had never actually taken any of them on.

In the same company, a fiction editor said that the rule was strictly observed.

Seven good reasons to have an agent

1 Some publishers (but certainly not all) won't look at unsolicited proposals. To be considered by them, you have to have an agent.

2 Some agents (but certainly not all) will help you hone your proposals and ideas to improve them and make them more saleable. They know what publishers respond well to, and can help make your submission more likely to be accepted.

3 Agents should know most editors personally – it's their business to. If they have a good relationship with the editor, then it will get a submission looked at more quickly and more favourably.

4 Having an agent means you don't have to do any touting of your proposal round the houses, you don't have to do any negotiating or administration, and you can concentrate on writing.

5 Agents sometimes know how to negotiate better financial terms than you could yourself, and are adept at playing publishers off against each other – if your main concern is just the money up front, this could be useful.

6 Good agents can bring work to you, if you are looking to write full time.

7 Agents know publishing contracts inside out and can quickly flag what's important and weed out any questionable clauses or wording.

Four reasons why the wrong agent might cause problems

1 **Some may not add any value**

There are agents who send a proposal to an editor with a covering letter that tells the editor in imperious tones that this is an outstanding book concept and that it will sell in huge volumes. In reality the proposal may well be poor and the editor really resents being presented with something that needs a lot of work to make it any good. Meanwhile the agent has probably told the author how great the proposal is, so that if the publisher tries to improve it, the author is taken aback and may be quite resistant. It happens.

Insider's view

One mass market non-fiction editor from a very large general publishing house tells of two areas where she feels very frustrated with some agents. "Structure of a proposal is important. If the actual writing needs close attention, that's OK. But if the structure is weird, that's the agent's job."

On a related point, this editor (like many others) gets really frustrated if a submission arrives that she can see could have been really good, but isn't. If she can see that a submission could have done with three more week's work, and would probably then have been accepted, then the agent is clearly not adding the value they should.

2 They may get in the way of a good dialogue

There are plenty of editors who would much rather cut out what they see as the middle man, and have a more productive direct relationship with the author.

3 They may nitpick over contracts

Putting the financial terms to one side, in the eyes of some publishers, agents needlessly and endlessly nitpick over every last word of the publishing contract. The agent would have you believe that they are protecting you the author from the evil blaggards in the publishing world who are out to trip you up, screw you out of every last penny and make you sign away your life. For most publishers this isn't true – if your business is built on attracting the best authors to publish with you, then conning, deceiving and generally diddling authors out of their entitlements or making their lives misery would be pretty bad PR. (If you can manage to contact some authors published by a particular company, you should soon find out what kind of publisher they are and whether you need to worry about contracts.)

It simply irritates the commissioning editor to have to argue over little points that really make no odds, but are time consuming and fiddly to have changed or cause logistical problems in house (just imagine a big publishing house trying to operate when every one of its thousands of authors had a completely different contract – it'd be mayhem).

4 They may see finances as the be all and end all

Going back to your reasons for being published, it may not be just about money for you. However, it's almost always about money for the agent – it's their business. It's possible that an agent could push the publisher to breaking point on every part of the finances, when for many other reasons they might be the best publisher for you. That publisher may eventually lose the will to live as a result of the never ending niggling over the foreign rights cut, and tell you to take the book elsewhere, when that rate is not what matters to you, the author.

The agent could also steer you towards whoever pays the most, when that might not be what's best for you. You might be better off with a publisher who doesn't offer the biggest advance or the highest royalty, but who will give you the best advice and support with developing your book or who is fantastic with organising speaking events or PR for you as a person, or whatever it is that you most value. The agent won't necessarily have this uppermost in their mind.

Case in point

The Managing Director of one small publisher relates how he offered a contract to an author, who was delighted. She decided to bring in an agent as she had plans for several books of different kinds, and thought she might as well secure an agent from the outset as this was her first book.

The agent was a nightmare for the publisher to deal with, being particularly nitpicky over every term. The MD happened to mention this to the author who was furious, as she had given him clear instructions that the terms were fine and not to push the agent as she was happy to go ahead. He had deliberately ignored her, and made life very difficult for the publisher in doing so.

What to remember if you decide to opt for an agent

Golden rule

If you do decide to get an agent, remember that they are acting for you.

This golden rule means that though you are wise to listen to their advice, you are not bound to accept it. You can and should give them instructions as to what is important to you, and what you would like them to do on your behalf. For example, you can instruct your agent not to niggle over small points of the contract, as you trust the publisher in question. Or that you'd like them to bring their contract points to you before taking them to the publisher so you can decide if all are important to you.

There are unscrupulous publishers, just as there are unscrupulous agents or unscrupulous accountants or unscrupulous people in any other profession or business. You do have to be careful which publisher you deal with, but if you are dealing with a decent company, and you are going to have an agent, please make sure they act in your best interests – which means you tell them what you want from the deal.

There is a middle way of course: to handle the submission and book discussions yourself and, if there's a contract offer, you can then bring in an agent to handle the discussion about legal and financial terms. Remember, you are the client – you can bring in an agent whenever you want. It is perfectly acceptable to ask an agent to represent you when you have an interested publisher and specify that if you want them to handle the administrative or financial side of contract negotiation only. They would be a bit silly not to as it's guaranteed money for them at that point.

The bottom line

There are agents who do add value and are brilliant advocates. In the course of researching this book I have spoken to agents whom I would be delighted to deal with as a publisher and whom I would be very proud to have represent me as an author. However, like all the editors I have talked to, I have come across agents who drive me nuts and really get my back up. I am compelled to tell the truth about agents from the publisher's view therefore and to issue a note of caution that not every agent will be the asset you assume they will be.

If you have written something that is so hot it's scorching, that nobody else could possibly write, if it's fiction or if you are an A list celebrity, an agent is probably a good idea as they may well get you the very best financial deal. If you've got a good non-fiction idea and want to work with a publisher to make it the best it can be, an agent might not always be your best option.

As a general rule, if you have one particular book you want to have published, know which publisher you'd be most happy with, and know they accept unsolicited submissions, an agent might be not necessary or desirable.

If your top choice publishers say they don't accept unsolicited proposals however, you should try and secure an agent to represent you. It's stacking the odds against you to try without.

Going it alone – sources of advice

If you have decided not to get an agent, then this book is designed to help you through the process of finding and approaching a publisher. Additionally, the basics of contracts are covered in Chapter 7. If you want more guidance on the contractual side of a publishing agreement, then the cheapest and best way is probably to join the Society of Authors, who will give you advice as to whether a financial proposition looks a fair one for the kind of book under consideration, and on the content of the contract. See pp.166-7 for more on getting advice on terms and contracts.

Other books on the subject, and sources of further information, are listed on the website at **www.whiteladderpress.com**.

Finding and securing an agent

If you've decided you want an agent, the next step is to find a good one and persuade them to represent you. This may not be as straightforward as it sounds. Agents are aplenty, but good ones are not so common, and persuading them to take you on can be difficult. A good agent is likely to represent a limited number of author clients, as they only have the capacity to handle so many to a high standard. The aim is to wow them with a compelling proposal in the same way you would wow a publisher (see Chapter 5).

But first, how do you go about finding the right agent to approach?

How to find a good agent

1 Know what you need from an agent

Do you need somebody to go over your proposal thoroughly and make it zing? Are you really happy with your written pitch but scared stiff of finance? Is it just the contacts you need? Agents are different in what they offer. I know an agent who is very up front about the fact that he really isn't very good at editorial improvements to book proposals, but he does have a first rate network of contacts in publishing and is fantastic at getting the best deal. On the other hand, an author I know tells me that her agent went into the minutiae of everything she had written, debated it with her, put it through a rigorous process of improvement, and only then proceeded to approach publishers. You need to think about what you need, and bear this in mind when you are looking for the right person to approach.

2 Personal recommendation

It's not always possible, but it's definitely the best way. If you believe in the 'six degrees of separation' rule then you will know somebody who knows somebody who either works in publishing or has had a book published and can give you personal feedback on who to approach. As we established above, the right agent for one person might not be the right person for another, so ask any contacts why the agent is good or bad. If it's an author, ask whether the agent improved the submission. Did they know exactly who to pitch to? Did they get a fantastic financial deal? Check this against what you think you need from an agent. If it's a publisher, ask who they like to deal with, or at least who they respect, even if the rest of the process pains them.

3 Association of Authors' Agents (AAA)

Members of the AAA have to have at least three years' experience under their belt. It's worth checking this as if anything does go wrong, you can go to the Association for help. Additionally, members use a standard agreement letter with their authors, giving you one less thing to worry about.

4 Track record

If you want to publish a literary novel, then it's worth looking at who represents writers you admire. If an agent has one great novelist in their care, it might be coincidence that the author picked them as an agent. If they have several, it suggests that they have a talent for picking (and maybe nurturing) great authors. Think of an author who you think has been well published, in a similar area to you, and then find out who their agent is. This is usually not too difficult – a bit of internet research is often all you need. Bigger authors will have their own websites and will tell you who their agent is there (as a test I found Andrea Levy's agent and his details in seconds). Otherwise doing an internet search on the author's name might bring up the agent's website – agents tend to make their list of clients public, after all.

5 **Research the agent**

Lists of agents can be found in *The Writers' and Artists' Yearbook/The Writer's Handbook* and on various websites for writers. Check what subject areas the agent works in – not all agents cover all areas and you are wasting your time if you send a submission for a book on keeping ferrets to an agent who only deals in crime novels. (Though it could be a whole new avenue of writing for you if they misunderstood and assumed it was a ferret crime book.) Look at the agent's website. Read as much about them as you can. What are they interested in? Do you like the sound of them? Does their client list fit? And very importantly, are they encouraging new authors to apply? How long do they take to respond? One agent's website (and one with a high profile agency too) said he would respond in a week and would read all submissions. That's quite astonishing! Some agents are sole traders and some work for a big agency. Generally I suspect more people apply to the bigger agencies, so a sole trader might make you one of fewer – however, agencies employ several agents and usually a few support staff who do reading for the agency, so I'm not sure the chances of your submission being picked up are any different overall.

6 **Find a way to interview the agent**

An agent should always invite you to meet them before taking you on as a client. I would never sign up with an agent I hadn't met. Use this as your opportunity to make sure you like them, and that you feel good about their ability to represent you. One editor said the best agents were all ones she could 'have a chat with' – so if you find this easy, chances are they will be a good people person with editors too.

Some agents, like publishers, don't take kindly to simultaneous submissions (see p.128). Be a bit careful here if there are particular agents you really like the sound of. I'd urge you always to read the website and submission guidelines.

Remember that agents only earn money if they are successful in selling you and your book. It's in their interests to help you create the most profitable book. If you have a choice of agent, listen carefully to the feedback on your submission from all of them. Don't go with an agent because they are a 'yes' man and rave about what you do. Look for the enthusiasm but also the most useful and constructive feedback.

> "The moments I cherish are when I give feedback to an author and I see the flash of comprehension in their eyes. I know then that I've already had a positive effect on that person's book."
> *Antony Topping, agent, Greene & Heaton Ltd.*

The final factor of course is that all important one. You need to find an agent who believes in you, and whom you believe in. No two agents are exactly the same, and finding somebody you trust and want to work with is important.

Ask them as many questions as you like before signing up. Discuss your book with them, of course, but I would also ask if they have a list of publishers in mind for your book, and chat those over. See how much the agent knows about the publisher and individual editors there. Has the agent sold books to that editor before? If so, this is useful as it means they will already have negotiated a standard (or boilerplate) contract with them, which is good for you and your book as the editor doesn't have to start from scratch with that agent (they will be pleased about that).

If an agent doesn't have a good list of potential editors to approach with a book, I would be wary. As one very scrupulous (and exemplary) agent said to me "Even if I liked a manuscript and had read the whole thing, if I didn't have a decent list of editors in mind to send it to, I would probably pass."

Signing up with an agent

If you reach the wonderful moment where you've found an agent you are really happy with, who wants to represent you, then there will be a standard letter of agreement that you will be asked to sign. It will probably include something about exclusivity – the agent will want to be your sole representative. The agreement is usually for an indefinite period, but should say that either side can terminate with a set period of notice (three months is the norm here). The normal understanding is that any books that the agent sells to a publisher on your behalf will stay with that agent, even if you subsequently end the agreement with them and go it alone, or with somebody else. In other words, for those books, the agent will continue to represent you and take their cut for doing so.

5 Writing a proposal

How to write what they want to read

A polished, professional and compelling first approach to the publisher or agent is absolutely vital. Nothing, but nothing is more important than your submission.

But how do you do it? What do they need to know? Do they want a full manuscript or one page outline? What is a synopsis exactly? What will get the editor's attention and what will turn them off instantly?

Small wonder that so many people find their burning idea in a dusty pile of A4 under the stairs 10 years later. It's no exaggeration to say one mistake here and you could mess up your chances of getting published for good.

Case in point

One writer, who now has over 50 books under his belt, relates how he spent the best part of two decades sending off proposals and submissions with absolutely no joy whatsoever. Then he met somebody who understood what made publishers and agents tick, and how to sell to them. He totally revised the structure and content of his proposals on their advice and since then almost every book proposal he's written has been accepted.

What to write

As you sit down to start drafting your submission, remember that you will be judged on both what you write and how you write it. You absolutely have to be compelling, concise and correct. You should come across as likeable and confident, ideally with just a touch of humility.

The investment of time and effort here needs to be considerable. You need not so much to write a submission as to craft it. Be prepared to plan it, draft it, read it, review it, rewrite it and so on. There's no room for slapdash.

So what exactly do you put down on paper?

Golden rule

Give the publisher or agent what they ask for.

Look at the website or the entry in *The Writers' and Artists' Yearbook/The Writer's Handbook* for the publisher or agent you want to approach. They will probably have submission guidelines. If they have, give them what they want. If you don't give them what they want, the best you can hope for is that they will just be mildly irritated by you when they read what you send. But more likely your book idea just won't get considered at all. If they ask for an enquiry letter initially, then that's exactly what you should send. A synopsis and three chapters, sent by email? You know what to do.

Whatever they ask for, remember before you put fingers to keyboard that editors and agents do not sit around all morning idly flicking through a couple of manuscripts, pausing to laugh here and make a note there before a long a boozy lunch that lasts most of the afternoon (oh I wish). They are generally heavily overworked professionals, struggling to keep their heads above paper. They may have spent most of the day in internal meetings, dealing with monstrous egos, dealing with admin and negotiating deals. Their attention span will be short. Their temper may well be shorter. There's no room for lengthy deliberation and pontification on your part – you have to hook them very quickly. At best you want them reaching for the phone to sign you up before the end of page one. At the very least you have to pique their interest enough to read on.

> "Most proposals that arrive here cross my desk. Many don't stop moving."
> *Ian Jackson, Editorial Director, Eddison Sadd*

Let's suppose that you've checked out the publisher or agent, and they aren't very specific about what you should send. Or that you want to try writing a proposal as practice. So how do you do it?

Here we need to divide into fiction and non-fiction, as this is where the major differences come into play.

Fiction

Ultimately, with fiction it's largely about your plot and your sample material. If an agent or publisher starts reading and is grabbed by your writing style and subject, then you're off to a great start. If they glance at your synopsis and it doesn't do anything for them, or if they start reading your first sample chapter and find it hard going or uninteresting, you're going to be rejected.

Your sample material therefore is of absolutely paramount importance. However, let's look at the whole package, as the sample material won't be the first thing the agent or editor sees on opening the envelope.

The first thing to stress is that there is no 'perfect' submission. Those that delight won't look exactly the same. However, the main components of a fiction submission are usually:

- Covering letter/email
- Synopsis
- Sample chapters

Covering letter

This isn't essential, but it's usual. It's your chance quickly to introduce yourself and your book to the editor or agent, and of course to get all your contact details in front of them, in the hope they will be used.

Whatever you do, don't make the classic mistake of just dashing off a note and sticking it on top of your sample chapters. You will be judged on your letter.

> "If you can't write a letter, you can't write a book."
> *Antony Topping, agent, Greene & Heaton Ltd.*

Topping suggests that you look at your letter as page 1 of your submission. A brilliant piece of advice. Make it brief, make it accurate and make it interesting. The aim of the covering letter is to have the editor or agent turn to the sample material feeling positive about you and your book.

Would-be authors make howling errors in their covering letters. If I sampled enough agents and publishers I'm sure we could fill a book of them in their own right. I can't cover everything in the 'what not to say' category, but here are a few pointers:

1 Write as you talk – the letter is from you, the person.

2 Don't be aggressive or arrogant.

3 Don't use flowery or archaic language. 'Please find enclosed herewith the completed manuscript for your perusal' is unlikely to go down well.

4 Don't include anything about confidentiality (see p.136).

5 Don't challenge the editor/agent. 'Are you the agent brave enough to take this mould breaking book on?' will just get the answer 'no'.

6 Don't go too far. 'I would expect Johnny Depp to be cast in the role of Ade in the film version of the book' is not going to help your case at all.

So what *do* you say in the covering letter?

In one page, simply tell the editor or agent in your own words what type of book it is (historical thriller? contemporary romance?), and what you are sending with the letter. Be polite with a touch of humility but not completely self-deprecating. Make it personal to them: if it's an agent, say you would like them to consider representing you, if it's a publisher then say you'd like them to publish your book. Say why you are sending it to that person if you can – good reasons would be that you know they represent/publish other authors/books that you admire.

If you say 'I am sending the book to you because you represented/published Jack Jones' *Liberty* and my book is in a similar vein' then be very careful you aren't namechecking a book that is now four years old and that wouldn't be published if it were proposed now because the market has changed. It's very important you demonstrate market awareness and that you aren't trying to 'jump on a hearse'.

There is no one single formula for a winning letter – it needs to be personal, but if you take the above dos and don'ts into account then you should be fine. Here's what one published author would write as a covering letter – she stressed it wouldn't necessarily work for everybody, but it should work for some:

> Dear Annie Agent
>
> I'd like to ask if you'd consider representing me for my novel *Circle of Five* (working title). It's a contemporary story of five women whose lives are intertwined by their children, or lack of them. The ability to have children, or not, is such a big issue for most women now, yet it hasn't been explored by many writers and I believe will strike a chord with thirtysomethings in particular. I see it as a novel for the *Desperate Housewives* market.
>
> I read the small biography of you that's on your website, and the areas of fiction you're especially interested in, and felt you'd be the kind of agent I'd love to have represent me. I'm enclosing a synopsis and the first three chapters. I hope you like them.
>
> Thanks for your time
>
> All best wishes
> Abbie Author

Synopsis

Interestingly, several of the agents and editors I spoke to don't actually read the synopsis or, if they do, certainly not first. One editor finds the synopsis 'hard to read' and prefers to judge a submission on the actual chapters themselves. Another doesn't like to know the full story in advance of reading the sample material as it means they can't read the novel with fresh eyes, as a reader opening it for the first time would do. Most editors and agents want to see if the book itself absorbs them.

However, you should send a synopsis anyway – it's there if the agent or editor wants to read it, and even those who don't like to read it first may look at it later. One agent told me he finds it useful to review the synopsis if he's read quite a lot of the manuscript and likes it, to check whether the author's view of the book tallies with his.

Editors and agents generally feel that well written synopses are few and far between, which is a pity as it's generally seen as important that a writer is capable of writing a précis of their own book.

Again, there is no single winning formula, but a possible structure for a synopsis would be:

- Brief description of the book
- A brief outline of the key characters
- A brief chapter by chapter summary (if you work like that) that shows what happens and how the plot develops, stage by stage
- A brief summary of you and your work to date

- Any other details or information that is relevant

Some say that the brief description of the book should be written like jacket copy (also known as cover blurb), but others caution that you shouldn't try too hard to make it sound like a publisher's blurb and that it should have your 'voice'.

Essentially, you are trying to make sure that in your covering letter and synopsis between them you cover the following:

- What the book is about
- Who the book is aimed at
- Why it should be published
- Proposed length of the book (in words)
- Suggested completion date (either months from acceptance, or a date)
- Where you have been published before (if you have)

Being able to 'elevator pitch' your book is a useful discipline to master for most types of book. (Elevator pitch refers to the situation where you are in a lift with a really important person and have just the time it takes to go up three floors to get your idea across.) See p.99 for guidance on how to do this. For what's known as 'high concept' fiction, it's essential by definition as this means the plot of the book can be described in a couple of sentences.

Sample manuscript

This is the crucial part of the submission. So long as the agent/editor hasn't been completely put off by your covering letter, they will start to read your sample chapters. And it's very simple then: either they don't like it, in which case they stop reading and reject your submission, or they are absorbed by it, in which case they keep on reading.

Most decide pretty quickly if the book is really not for them. It has to be that way – you couldn't read hundreds of submissions a year if you spent ages on each one. A few pages are normally enough to know if it's really not for you. The ideal outcome is summed up best of all by agent Antony Topping, "You're on the tube in the evening on your way to meet friends and you've opened a first chapter to read. Suddenly you realise you've been totally transported to another world and without realising it you're already on page 15."

Whether or not this happens will of course be totally dependent on your writing ability and your storyline.

> "I think one of the most important things is not to try to be the new somebody else. Write in your own voice; that's what's charming and what's unique. I read so many books and feel they've been written to a formula. Be brave. When you write in your own voice you're exposing yourself."
> *Marian Keyes, bestselling author*

So, how much of your book do you send? Some agents and editors say send three chapters, others say just make sure the total number of pages isn't more than 100. A small amount is the general guideline. There are just two golden rules here:

1 Don't send your whole manuscript. Almost all would see it as a waste of paper and unnecessary. If the reader gets to the end of the third chapter and is still reading, believe me they will definitely contact you to ask for the rest.

2 Always send the beginning of the manuscript – Chapters 1-3 say. Whatever you do, don't send Chapters 3, 5 and 7. There's nothing more self-destructive than saying 'I've sent Chapter 3 as that's where it gets interesting.'

Knowing you are going to be judged pretty quickly might make it tempting to overdo the opening chapters. Don't go over the top and make them overwrought, just make sure there's enough there to keep the reader's interest.

> **Insider's view**
>
> Most agents and editors don't read new submissions during the working day. They are too busy with day to day business issues for that. New submissions are often read in the evenings and at weekends. Make sure that what you send will make their spare time happily spent.

If you are preparing your submission, and at this point you've only written the sample chapters, you need to stop and think for a minute. What if the agent or publisher calls you and says they are really interested in your sample material, could you please send the whole manuscript, as you've said it is complete? Supposing you said it's complete and it isn't? You really are in a tricky position. They aren't going to be best pleased when you get back to them to say that actually you exaggerated slightly and would six months to write it be OK? You may well have lost them then. Equally you don't want to be in a position that you have to write through the night every night for three weeks to finish the book. It's hardly likely to be your best work.

Author Laura James suggests that you should be aware of the consequences of sending in the outline and sample material, when that's all you've done, "The agent or publisher is effectively like an investor on the futures market – they are investing in your book in anticipation that they will earn returns in the future. If you haven't written the book yet and you tell an agent or publisher this, you are effectively inviting them to get involved with the crafting of the book, to try and make their gamble as low risk as possible. This might be brilliant, particularly if you're a first time author, but then again it might not."

Either way, writing the whole novel before sending seems like the best option. It means that you might have some revision and rewriting to do in the light of feedback from the agent or publisher, but that's a nice kind of problem to have.

Editorial services

Before submitting your novel to an editor or agent, you might be thinking about using a reading/editorial service either to critique or to edit your sample chapters. Lists of individuals and companies that offer this kind of service appear in *The Writers' and Artists' Yearbook/The Writer's Handbook* or can be found using a quick web search.

Obviously the value of a critique depends on the ability of the reader and their experience. Tread carefully, and ask for references. There is no guarantee that everybody offering these services knows what agents and editors are actually looking for – so make sure before you pay for this kind of help that the person is well qualified to offer it.

Enquiry letters

Some agents and publishers suggest you send an enquiry letter first. In many ways this seems odd, as surely a novel can only be judged by whether it's well written or not? Maybe, but if that's what they ask for, you can only assume that's what they want. If requested, send an enquiry letter along the lines of the covering letter on p.85, outlining in a few sentences the subject of the book and any other key information. An enquiry letter might also say something about you, if there's something relevant to say (such as where you've been published before, if you have). One agent suggests you say something about yourself that also positions your work by mentioning which authors you admire and have influenced you. This has dual benefit: firstly it tells the agent or editor that you read widely and have thought about how your book sits in the spectrum of published books. Secondly, in an oh-so-humble way, it hints at possible benchmarks. 'Writers I particularly admire and who have influenced me include Martin Amis' comes across so much better than 'I write like Martin Amis.'

Fiction – getting published against the odds

Fiction is undoubtedly fiercely competitive. It's also critical that you deal with rejection in the right way (see p.191). You need to have real commitment to success as it's probably going to be a tough ride. Before you set out, be as sure as you can that you have something saleable, and that you really do want this. Even bestselling, well published novelists suggest you think twice before going ahead. One commented to me that she would seriously try and deter people from trying to get their novel published "there are far, far too many of them and most are bad… the majority only sell about 300 copies." That said, the lucky, successful few who do get their first fiction work published each year will probably be very glad they persevered.

Children's fiction

Unfortunately, many would-be authors seem to think that writing a children's book is a bit of a doddle. You wonder if the thought process is something like this: 'Only 20 pages, and just one line of text on each page – how hard can it be?' Children's publishers will tell you quite clearly that writing for children is not easier than writing for adults. And every editor will tell you that writing less is much much harder than writing more. This applies to adult books as well as children's. Be warned that children's publishers get absolutely deluged with book ideas, many from parents who make up stories for their children and then think it would be fun to get them published. Madonna had the advantage of being A list – don't forget that.

Before you even put pen to paper to write your proposal, do some serious thinking.

- Are you sure you can write? Have you read and learned about the craft (there are lots of good books about writing for children)? Have you practised?
- What age are you writing for? You have to have a very precise reader in mind, in age terms. Booksellers and publishers categorise children's books by age of child. Who is yours for? It must be stated in your proposal.
- Are you sure you understand the mind of the child at that age? If

your own child is your chief guinea pig, are you sure they're typical for their age?

- Have you read a lot of books aimed at children of that age? Have you studied the level of writing, the characters used, the range of vocabulary?

If you're satisfied that you have, and you are very clear about what you are doing, then it's time to get the concept down on paper. Make sure in everything you write that you are conveying that you are clear exactly who your reader is, and that you have done your research. Most importantly in what you write is you mustn't come across as an amateur, in either your proposal or your covering letter. 'My children really liked this when I read it to them' isn't a good line. You are a writer who understands children, not a parent who thinks they can write.

There is a series of fabulous interviews with published children's authors at The Word Pool website (**www.wordpool.co.uk** – see Author Profiles). It's well worth reading all of the profiles as not only do the published writers share their experiences of getting published, but also how they find their inspiration and how they write. Several messages come through loud and clear, especially the importance of talking with children, researching your market and practice (lots of it).

Children's fiction should be proposed using the general fiction guidelines on p.82.

If it's a children's non-fiction book you are thinking of, then you need to absorb the general information above on writing for children, and then use the following section to craft a proposal.

Non-fiction

The pitch of the non-fiction book is absolutely critical. I can't stress this strongly enough. You need to spend as much time and effort on the actual proposal itself as on your sample chapter/material. You need to think like a copywriter, do your research, plan the whole document out in advance and then make sure it's as compelling and clear as it can possibly be. And you need to get your pitch across in the minimum number of words. Waffling is a heinous crime.

Author turned publisher Roni Jay suggests the first thing you do before writing anything down is to think very hard about whether there is a market for the subject you've got in mind before you think about whether your book is the right one for that market. Being able to think in these terms is part of your job as a writer, especially of non-fiction. Only when you're sure there is a market and that your book is the right one to meet the need should you proceed to the next stage. It will save you endless time and wasted energy.

Hopefully, you'll be doing this planning phase before you've written the manuscript. If not, and you've already written it, whatever you do, resist the temptation to forget a proposal and send the whole manuscript. There are three main reasons for this:

1. There's a very strong chance it won't get read and you've wasted paper and postage.

2. What editors really want is a short sharp proposal. A lot of paper at this stage can make them feel quite sick.

3. Many non-fiction publishers are actually put off a book if it's already written. I'm not alone in always being happier to take on

> a book on the basis of an outline and some sample text. It means I can help guide the author on the structure and content and scope, and ensure it will be exactly as I want it to be. If the whole book is written, you are risking that the editor likes it exactly as it is, or is willing to invest the considerable time and effort into giving detailed feedback and working with you while you rework the manuscript if necessary. Most editors will tell you that it's usually very difficult to persuade an author to rewrite a book once it's written.

It's definitely a very bad idea indeed to send just a whole manuscript with a covering letter that says 'here's my book, do you want to publish it?' If an editor or agent drowning in paper sees a huge manuscript arrive on their desk as the initial contact, the reaction is likely to be an immediate groan. You're effectively asking a really busy person to have to work hard from the outset to find out what your book is about and who it's for. You've got to make it easy for them. As easy as possible.

For non-fiction, the most valuable document you can write is a brief, succinct proposal. Your first contact is largely about pitching the concept. The editor or agent will be able to assess interest very quickly from a concise pitch. If they think they might be interested, then they will come back to you and ask for more material, and specify exactly what they would like to see.

Insider's view

The terms proposal and synopsis are often used interchangeably. Although actually even the term synopsis is interpreted differently by different people – some use synopsis to refer to just the outline of the story/content, and others take it to mean the outline plus a description of the market and other factors also.

The big difference between a fiction synopsis and what I refer to as a non-fiction proposal is that the proposal covers much more than what's in the book. The element of pitching is significant, as is positioning, competition analysis and addressing why it will sell.

One editor I talked to said his ideal first contact was a simple one pager stating what the book is about, who it's for, why they will buy it and who you are. If he's interested, he will then send the person guidelines as to what else he wants to know. For me, and others, one page is possibly a bit on the short side – the optimum first contact for me is probably 2–4 pages of proposal with a small amount of accompanying sample text, but I agree that it should be concise and very tightly pitched. Editors and agents do decide very quickly if they are interested or not. The shorter, more compelling pitch you can write, the better.

If in doubt, I'd suggest a covering letter or email, a 2–4 page proposal and a sample of the manuscript (introduction probably) if you have one. Many agents and publishers have their own proposal guidelines – check the website and, if they exist, use them. If not, or if you want to prepare a generic synopsis or proposal that you can then adapt to each publisher's requirements, then I offer below a couple of different templates for the content and structure of a good proposal.

Thinking through your book idea using the headings provided should be enormously helpful to you in testing your idea rigorously.

You need to be able to answer these questions fully and clearly, whether they are in that publisher's guidelines or not. This process can turn a half- baked idea into a really clear and compelling one.

Writing a non-fiction proposal

The objective of the proposal is twofold:

1 To sell your book idea.
2 To sell you as the author.

The proposal should set out what the book is about and – most importantly – why it will sell. It should also provide evidence that you have the necessary knowledge to write the book, and that you can write well. These things should be uppermost in your mind at all times. Remember – be clear, be compelling and be correct.

A good editor will read your proposal in two ways (either consciously or unconsciously). They will read it from the point of view of a publishing professional. They will also read it as a potential bookshop browser.

Questions the editor will be asking with their publisher's hat on

- What's the market?
- How big is the market?
- Where's the need for the book?
- Does it offer a promise of more success and happiness, or is will it entertain, inform or inspire?

- Does the author have the ability and qualifications to write the book?
- What's the competition? Is this different?
- If there's a lot of competition, are we looking at competing for a small piece of the pie, or can we take away sales from somebody else?
- If it's new and original, or an emerging subject, are we at the right point of the 'wave' – not too early or too late?

Questions the editor will be asking with their reader's hat on

- Would I pick this off the shelf?
- What's it going to do for me?
- Is it compelling? Would I go straight to the till after reading the description?

You have to include information that satisfies both your publisher and your eventual reader. The way I suggest constructing the proposal allows you to write copy that pitches the book to the reader, but also includes all the information that a publisher will need to cover the market information and the publishing rationale.

If you are in doubt what kind of language to use, I advise that you 'write as you talk' – if you wouldn't say something in conversation, don't write it down that way. This guarantees it will be easy to read and absorb and you are making the editor's job as straightforward as possible.

Remember the publisher is interested in what people will want to read, not what you can write. (Sorry, I know I have said this before, but it is important.) They aren't necessarily the same thing. Whatever you do don't take up half your proposal talking about you and why you're keen to write about this subject. The emphasis of the proposal has to be firmly on the reader and what they want to read. And while we're on the seven deadly sins of proposals, here's another: be very wary of saying things like 'this book should be read by x, y and z'. Books don't sell because they should be read. They sell because people want to read them or feel they need to read them. I'm always very cautious if I see a book described as, let's say 'something every middle aged man should read'. Contrast this with a book pitched as 'the book that every middle aged man will be desperate to read' – that's another story altogether…

The art of pitching

There's no doubt about it, the ability to pitch your ideas well is a fine art. Whether it's in your proposal or in your covering letter, if you can say something short and sweet so the editor 'gets it' immediately, it's half the battle over. If you've a background in advertising or copywriting, you'll be ahead of the game, but if you're a mere mortal and have the time and inclination, it's worth dipping into some good copywriting books to master the art of the descriptive soundbite. I've suggested a few in the further reading section on the website.

The wonderful Richard Stagg, an Editorial Director who has pitching, soundbites, titles and straplines down to a fine art has his favourite example of 'high concept' pitching, from the film industry.

The film *Alien* was apparently pitched like this:

Alien = Jaws in space

That's perhaps taking it to extremes, but you can see how a good snappy soundbite can do the work of five pages of description.

Many Hollywood films, including *Gladiator*, were pitched in a paragraph. It's a good discipline for books as well as films – fiction and non-fiction.

The proposal structure and content

Here I offer some different ways of structuring a non-fiction proposal. The first is my preferred way:

Give yourself the following headings and craft your content under them accordingly. Then you can take most of the headings out, or give them your own headings. They are intended as guidance on what you should cover, not an absolutely rigid structure.

- Title
- Subtitle
- 10 second sell (aka elevator pitch, aka 'in a nutshell')
- Headline bullet points on why the book will sell
- Brief outline
- Market
- Competition/benchmarks
- Contents list
- Author biography

Title

A title is pretty important. Not perhaps as important as you might think, because it can be changed by the publisher (usually with your agreement, but not always – contractually the publisher normally has the final say on the title), but you need to put something on the proposal. Be very careful here. A bad title can put off a publisher. You should already have looked at that publisher's list and know what kinds of title they go for. If they go for straight to the point titles (the ones I call 'Ronseal' titles because they 'do what it says on the tin') then it's probably best not being obscure or irreverent. Generally in non-fiction the best advice is: if in doubt, go for a fairly descriptive/obvious title. In fiction and children's books there's clearly more leeway.

Insider's view

Sometimes when a proposal lands on our desks the lack of a great title isn't a problem, as the right one immediately springs to mind, or we know there's time to create one. Sometimes, however, it's the missing link and we know that if we can't get the title right, the book will die, so we need to crack it before we can go any further…

If you aren't convinced by your title, consider adding 'working title' in brackets after the title. It shows that you know it might not necessarily be the right title and demonstrates that you are open to it being changed – both of which are good signs for the editor or agent. Equally, try not to be too attached to a title, even if you love it.

Here are a few examples of what I consider to be brilliant titles, and why (sadly for you, these are all published books so can't be used):

Getting to Yes

For a book on negotiation, you couldn't get a better title. It's genius. The title instantly tells you what the book is about and also conveys the outcome of the book for the reader.

Babies for Beginners

This title manages to convey exactly what the book is about and at the same time gives a reassuring feeling. It's slightly unconventional compared to the other baby book titles which reflects the book – it gets across instantly that it will tell you what you really need to know about babies.

You Are What You Eat

Familiar phrase, summarises what the book is about, short, snappy and memorable. Winner.

Outwitting Dogs

Immediately stands out from the standard 'how to train your dog' books with a clever title. Will instantly appeal to those who like the idea of being the boss (men) and those who don't like the idea of brute force (women). Very clever and with a 'how to' subtitle it works really well. The only thing I personally would have done would be to call it 'Outwitting Your Dog' thus making it more personal.

What God Wants

For any religious book browser this is an instant hit. Again it's compelling, memorable and gives you a strong indication of what's in the book. It also promises to answer a big question or reveal a secret – always a good idea.

Making Bread at Home

Couldn't be simpler really. But it works.

It's usually not a good idea to be too derivative of a big selling title when sending yours in. Since the monumental success of Covey's *7 Habits of Highly Effective People*, publishers in the area have been deluged with proposals with titles and subtitles that are close variants. Think about why great titles worked and then apply the principles to your book.

See p139 for the legal issues regarding titles.

Subtitle

A subtitle and/or strapline is useful in making the book compelling. For most non-fiction books you will probably want to think about the outcome of the book. Why would somebody buy it? Then craft a subtitle that relates to the reason they will buy it. A diet or exercise book for example would have a subtitle that stresses how the book will give you a flat stomach, or lose you 7lbs or similar. Here are some possibilities and examples that I've just made up:

- A book about card tricks
  'how to impress your audience and improve your sleight of hand'

- A book on fundraising
  'how to raise lots of money for your charity'

- A concise history of the world
  'everything you need to know about world history, at your fingertips'

10 second sell (aka the elevator pitch, 'in a nutshell')

This is a critical part of the book proposal. It's really worth spending a while on crafting this. If you get it right, this couple of sentences could be all you need to sell the book.

The idea is that if you only had 10 seconds to describe what the book is about and who it's for, what it will do for them and why they would buy it, this is what you would say. I usually write these as if I am selling the book to the reader. It helps the editor see how they could sell it to their sales colleagues and how the reps could sell it to the bookstores and how the marketers could sell it to the reader.

This kind of pitch can be used all the way down the line and that's why it's so important. Increasingly, the publisher's sales reps are given very little time to sell an individual book to the retailer. Especially in the (rapidly decreasing) chains where reps sell to individual stores rather than to head office only. Hence the 10 second sell becomes more important than ever. Many is the book that has failed because it took too long to explain. If you can't pitch it quickly to the publisher, they will worry they can't pitch it quickly to the bookstore.

Here are some examples of what 10 second sells might look like:

The Green Superwoman

You want to be eco-friendly and do your bit to save the planet. But you've also got too much to do and not enough time to do it in. This is the first handy bitesize guide to being green at the speed of life. It's Shirley Conran's *Superwoman* for the recycling generation.

The Tales of Anglo and Saxon

Discover what life was like in 500BC through the eyes of Anglo the cat and Saxon the dog. A fascinating illustrated historical guide that five to seven year olds will love.

The Flyfishing Handbook

Fly fishing takes an hour to learn but a lifetime to master. This book is your companion for the hour and the lifetime, taking you from basic know-how to understanding the finer behavioural points of the adversary underwater. No tackle bag is complete without it.

Insider's view

The proposal starts with a really catchy title and subtitle. I know immediately who it's for and what it's offering. After reading the 10 second sell I know exactly what the reader will be getting from the book. Already I'm hooked....

Headlines bullet points on why the book will sell

This can be anything from the size of the market, to the need of the market, to how you will help promote and sell the book, to other books that are really selling well and how your book serves the same market. These are really important. You're aiming to grab the agent or publisher by convincing them in a few succinct lines that the book will sell. Here are some examples of what you might say:

- 400,000 people start a business each year in the UK alone – it is a large market, very hungry for good quality information.
- This will be the first book on complementary therapies that covers an exhaustive range of physical and mental conditions – it is truly encyclopaedic and will be the one book that every therapist has to have on their shelves.
- The author is a journalist with contacts at all the broadsheets. She has already gained commitment for articles on this topic to coincide with the book's publication.
- Thimble collecting is the fastest growing sector of 'antiques and collectables' – the publisher of the first illustrated guide will have considerable market advantage.

Brief outline

Three or four paragraphs describing the book in compelling sales/marketing copy. Again, you are trying to make it easy for the commissioning editor to say yes. Some advise writing this as if it were the jacket copy – direct it at the reader and describe what the book is, what it covers and why they will want to buy it.

Market

Who is going to buy it? How many of them are there? What else do you know about them? Where are they? Can they easily be reached? The more data that you can fit in here, the better. Use the internet to research statistics. If you can't find out how many thimble collectors there are, then insert the circulation figures of the leading antiques and collectibles magazines, and quote from the magazines about the rising interest in thimbles.

Say where the market is – is it purely UK? Is it global? Be honest, but do highlight overseas markets if there are any.

Is the market price sensitive? Think about their spending power. If the market is relatively small, you can offset this by stressing here that they are willing to pay over the odds for books offering top quality information.

What do they read? Where do they congregate? Are they generally known as good bookbuyers? It's really important you think about this.

Case in point

Will the market buy the book? One would-be author wanted to write a book of careers advice, specifically aimed at students while still at university. Her proposal simply mentioned that the book was for students and stated how many hundreds of thousands of students there were in the UK. What she hadn't considered at all is whether the students had any spending power, or whether they would choose to spend their ever mounting debt money on a book of careers advice or on a couple of pints and a kebab. Again, what others think a market should buy and what they actually will buy are often two different things.

Put yourself in the mind of the market. Is this really what they want? Ideally, when you've drafted your proposal, read it imagining you were reading it out loud to a person who represents your target market. What do they say? Does what you're proposing make sense to them?

Some authors list primary, secondary and even tertiary markets (especially more academic books). I'm not a big fan of this. The people who will buy the book are in the 'primary' category and the others are people who might buy the book but probably won't. If we can't count on them, we can't really factor them in.

Competition

You must be accurate and you must be honest. Search amazon for books with the same or similar titles to yours. If you can't find any book with the same title, try thinking about what words a reader might associate with the topic and search amazon for those words too. List all the main titles that come up as competition, with author, publisher, price and publication date (all can be found on amazon). Get hold of a copy of the main ones, have a read and a think about what's good and bad about them. In your proposal, give a two line summary of the key competition and a couple of lines on how your book differs.

I would always be honest about competitive books – if they are good in some respects, I would say so. Equally flag up the shortcomings.

Insider's view

It's really irritating when a submission contains the claim that there is no competition. This means that I have to do all the work in checking out what the competition is – price, level, content and how the proposed book differs. That is if I have the time or energy to do so, rather than just rejecting it. The proposal that contains a clear summary of the competition leaves me delighted as it's saved me a job and it demonstrates the author has really thought about where their book fits. A very good sign indeed.

Just because a book has competition, it doesn't mean that a publisher will be put off. There are so few truly original new ideas that doing things differently or better is a perfectly acceptable publishing strategy. In fact, it may be that if a particular publisher doesn't have a book on a topic, and all its competitors do, they will be quite keen to fill the gap in their list.

Case in point

I once commissioned a book for which there were at least half a dozen directly competing titles. I did it because I thought they were all poor. I looked out for the right author and when I found him, we planned how to knock the socks off the existing books in content, pitch and packaging. The book became the bestseller on the topic within six months and is still the bestseller today.

Make sure you don't do a demolition job on the competition if it is clearly selling really well. It suggests you have a very skewed view of the world.

Benchmarks

What kind of book do you want yours to emulate? This can be a book in the same field or a completely different area. If you give a benchmark you aren't saying that your book is the same as the one you mention – you are giving an example of the kind of book it is, or the kind of level it's at, or how another book defined a genre in the way you'd like yours to. A good way of putting it might be something like: 'my book is to erotic fiction what *The No. 1 Ladies Detective Agency* is to crime novels'. Or 'A good benchmark would be *Built to Last* – a very engaging, well told factual book.'

Contents list

This is where it's easy to be too brief or far too detailed. The trick here is to include just enough information that the editor or agent can see what broadly the book will cover, and how it will be broken down, without almost writing the book in the process.

A list of obscure chapter titles that don't tell you anything about the book, supported by no explanation is next to useless.

I would advise chapter titles, if relevant, and a brief paragraph explaining what each covers. Ideally this should take no more than a page of A4 – maybe less.

Author biography

The editor or agent does want to know something about you. View the biography as an opportunity to sell yourself, just as you've sold your book idea. It's not intended to be a character description, or a potted history of all your life events. It should be one or two paragraphs ideally, of the most relevant information.

Golden rule

Don't send a CV as a biography

Even if it's an academic book, you can work your academic credentials into the couple of paragraphs about you. There is definitely such a thing as too much information.

The main purpose of your biography in non-fiction is to clarify why you are qualified or suitable to write this book. It should mention relevant experience or credentials, research you've done or interests that have a bearing on the book.

Case in point

One editor at a large general publishing house tells of how he received a proposal for a book about the influences on and pressures of childhood today. It all looked good until the editor got to the author biography. It turned out that the author was solely basing her book on interviews with eight children. The author was neither an authority, nor had she done or intended to do any proper research. It was immediately rejected.

For example, here are a couple of fictitious biographies that would work for me:

***John Jones** is a mountaineer and climbing instructor. From his first climb, aged six, on an English gritstone edge, to the successful ascent of all 14 of the world's 8000m peaks, climbing has been his love and passion. John has contributed articles to most of the leading climbing magazines, including The Edge and Overhang. He is a regular speaker to climbing audiences all over Europe.*

***Alexandra Fenham** is a fully qualified aromatherapist, massage therapist and midwife. She was one of the early pioneers of the use of complementary therapies in pregnancy and childbirth, and has done several well quoted studies on the use of therapies to treat sleeping difficulties and minor medical conditions in babies. She is a council member of the Midwives' Research Association.*

Alexandra has four children of her own, and therefore has very personal experience of the benefits of complementary therapies in raising happy, healthy children.

Insider's view

I always look at a biography for evidence that the author has 'earned the right' to be the author of a book. I would never take on an author for a book on starting a business, say, if the would-be author had never started a business. There are some types of book that I'd accept from a non-expert, but I'd need to be very sure they had done (or were intending to do) suitable research and that their reasons for wanting to write the book seemed sensible. A real sense of passion for writing that particular book is always an asset.

The other thing I always look for is evidence that the author has a good network and will be a useful asset in promoting and selling their own book. This really swings in their favour.

An alternative very simple proposal structure

If you want to keep it really simple, you can always use fewer headings, as follows:

- Title and subtitle
- Overview
- Contents list with chapter breakdown
- Short author biography

This is only going to work if the premise for the book is really exceptionally strong. The overview would contain the rationale for the book (who it's aimed at and why they will buy it) as well as a description. The success of this approach totally depends on how well you express yourself in making this case.

Another alternative – a bit more risky

This is a method that one writer swears by. I'd say this one was pretty risky, but it works for him:

The first page of your proposal contains just the title and three very strong bullet points to describe the book's potential that will grab the editor. The second page then follows up with a few 'questions' posed to the editor:

"Did you know that there are 340,000 practising Quakers worldwide?"

"Did you know that the Quaker church is 350 years old next year and there will be a great deal of celebration and additional focus as a result?"

This is then followed by the usual outline of content of the book.

If you are going to try and pique the interest of the agent or editor in this way, you have to be pretty sure that you aren't being patronising and that you are genuinely flagging up something they didn't know already. Tone is important here too.

The 3Ps

An alternative to the 'why it will sell' bullet points and brief description is to use the 3Ps. This is also a useful technique if you need to summarise the book idea and the need and the market all in a very concise way. It ensures you are telling the editor everything they need to know, quickly and simply.

Position – set out what the situation is at present
Problem – explain why this situation isn't ideal
Proposal – what you intend to do about it

So, for example:

Position

Increasingly small charities are having to do their own fundraising as they can't afford to pay a professional fundraiser. They are looking to books for guidance on how to do it.

Problem

Most books on fundraising are either too basic, and don't give sufficient detail on how to go about each option, or give very detailed guidance on one aspect of fundraising (eg relationship fundraising).

Proposal

This book is a practical, easy to read handbook aimed at the small charity looking to do its own fundraising. The fundraising areas are broken down into strategies and techniques, with step by step guidance on how to go about each, how much you can expect to raise, handy tips for success and pitfalls to watch out for.

Seven things you should not say in a proposal, ever

1 'My book is like Harry Potter only better'

You can substitute any whopping seller in place of Harry Potter, depending on what your book is about. There are lots of reasons for this – you can probably guess many of them. Firstly, the editor or agent will have read the same thing countless times before. It just gets boring. It doesn't make your submission stand out at all. Secondly, chances are it isn't better than Harry Potter. Immediately the editor is thinking 'I doubt it' or 'Oh heavens not another one.' So you've got negative reactions going already. Same goes for saying 'My novel is like *The Da Vinci Code* only better written'. Even if the editor thinks like you that *The Da Vinci Code* isn't well written, that line isn't selling the book to them. See the advice on tackling benchmarks above.

2 There is no competition'

Yes there is. Or at least, I bet there is. Only in fiction can you possibly claim there is no competition – and even then of course you could argue there is, because there are plenty of novels to choose from. If you can't find any book on exactly the same subject, then the question to ask is 'What would my target market browser buy at the moment?' – that's your competition.

3 Slag off the publisher's existing books

This one may have you scratching your head in disbelief that anybody would. Oh but they do! For example, I have received covering letters proposing new mass market business books that state 'all business books are boring… so here's one that isn't.'

Three points here:

Firstly, the author is unlikely to have read every business book. In fact I suspect he's read very few. I now think he's prone to sweeping generalisations and exaggeration. If he had said x and y books were boring then fine I might have agreed. Then again, I might not.

Secondly, just because he has found a book boring, it doesn't mean that everybody has. He clearly believes that his view is The Truth. That annoys me. I find some books really boring, but I know not everybody does.

Finally, I publish business books. Therefore, by saying all business books are boring, he is telling me I publish boring books. Clearly, I am unlikely to think all my books are boring.

4 Go on (and on)

In particular, don't write too much background. The editor really isn't going to be interested in the exact circumstances that led to you deciding to write this book. Are you writing something because it's useful for the editor or because you want to write it? Brevity is good. Keep it tight.

5 Exaggerate or lie

Don't say you are lined up for a TV role, if actually you've just had a chat with a TV producer. Don't say you can get your book endorsed by Prince Charles, if you just know somebody who used to work at Highgrove. If the editor is interested in your book and a bit of quizzing reveals discrepancies, they might wonder what else you haven't been entirely straight about.

6 Patronise the editor

I don't think authors do this on purpose. But a sizeable minority does it anyway. You have to remember when you write the proposal, and especially the covering letter, that the editor believes they are the expert at knowing what is and isn't likely to sell. Telling them their job will really not help your cause. It is a fine balancing act between confidence and arrogance but you have to find it.

7 Be weird

It's hard to say whether people who come across as a bit weird in their proposal do it to stand out or whether they are on the far end of the behavioural spectrum.

Five ways to make it easy for them to say yes

1 **Write a good proposal** Spell check it (you wouldn't believe those

who don't) and proof it to ensure it makes sense. Craft your descriptive copy carefully. If you provide a proposal that they hardly even have to tweak to take forward, it makes it easy for them.

2 **Provide supporting evidence** Offer market data.

3 **Use good benchmarks** Help them share your vision.

4 **Show why you'll be a good author** Realistic expectations, an ability to write, a willingness to be flexible and lots of good ideas all help here.

5 **Demonstrate that you've thought about ways to reach the market or get publicity** – preferably in ways that mean you'll be taking some of the initiative.

Sample manuscript

If you are sending a sample of the manuscript and have been asked for 30 pages, don't send the first 30 pages if that includes 10 pages of acknowledgements and the like. In fact I wouldn't include the acknowledgements even if you are sending the whole manuscript – they might be offputting. If the small sample you are sending is mostly the guff that goes in the front of the book, it will try the patience of the reader. Get to the real text and leave the rest behind.

Covering letter/email

A covering letter isn't at all necessary in non-fiction, so long as all your contact details are on the proposal somewhere. However, if you are submitting by email, then of course you have to say something by way of introduction – an empty email just with an attachment looks seriously odd and might make the recipient nervous of opening the attachment.

Remember that the primary aim of the covering note is to encourage the editor to read the attached proposal or synopsis. Don't say too much, just make it simple and polite and write only enough to whet the appetite. Ideally, mention something about you that is a clear differentiator and will make you stand out, but nothing that will make you seem weird. Author Laura James recommends that you mention whether you have already been published in your covering letter, but don't scrape the barrel, "Don't mention the parish magazine if that's the only place you have been in print."

Special golden rule

Always, always, always (you can tell this one matters to me) put ALL your contact details on your covering letter and on the submission itself. Make it easy for the editor or agent to contact you how THEY want to...

There's a list of the lines you should never say in covering letters for fiction on p.84.

Poetry

Poetry is especially difficult to have published in book form and so warrants a special mention. There's little money to be made from poetry, which is the reason that most larger publishers no longer publish it. There are however a few that do, and plenty of smaller poetry publishers. There's little or no point submitting poetry collections to reputable publishers until you've built up a substantial portfolio of published poems in highly regarded magazines. Concentrate your early efforts on getting good coverage on websites, magazines and e-zines. Think about self publishing some of your own work, either via your own website or in book form (see Chapter 10). Enter competitions also – this is extremely useful in getting published.

Before submitting to a publisher, build your reputation, not only through magazine and web publishing, but also through writing and poetry groups. Networking and profile building are very important in getting published in poetry. With luck, a good poetry publisher might notice you this way too.

If you decide to submit a collection to a publisher, send a good covering letter (as for fiction), plus a summary of your publishing history that details all your magazine successes. Send with it the number of poems requested by the publisher – usually 10-30 (check the publisher's website).

Selling yourself to an editor

Don't forget when you are proposing a book to a publisher, that you are not just selling your idea. For most types of publishing, you're also selling yourself. Ideally you want the editor to like you. Everybody wants to work with people they like, or at the very least are pleasant to work with. Part of the joy of publishing (and being an agent) is working with brilliant people. It pays therefore to think very carefully about how you come across in everything you say and write. Your tone, manner and choice of words gives away so much more than you probably realise, and might prejudice an editor in favour of, or against, your book.

A very smart boss of mine once sketched a grid like this to show how authors can be one of four types:

MAINTENANCE \ IMPACT	High	Low
High	Great books, great sales, pain to work with	Average books, average sales, pain to work with
Low	Great books, great sales, joy to work with	Average books, average sales, but don't cause much stress

High Impact, High Maintenance

These are the authors you just have to live with as a publisher. You might not like them, they might cause you hell by being irritating, arrogant, childish, by changing their minds endlessly, by being eternally dissatisfied ('I've just been to a bookshop in Ethiopia and was appalled to discover they only had one copy of my book. I expect this to be dealt with immediately'), but they are good authors and their books sell, so you put up with it.

High Impact, Low Maintenance

These authors are a publisher's dream. They come up with great ideas, they write great books, they play an active part in promoting and selling their book. Yet they are lovely people, with no unreasonable expectations. This is the air you need to exude from every pore.

Low Impact, Low Maintenance

This kind of author doesn't excite a publisher, but if you aren't going to be a three Nurofen a day kind of author to work with, the publisher is more likely to take a punt on you and your book. This doesn't mean you can afford to come across as unsure or vague. Confidence is key. The author who seems confident without wanting the moon on a stick has the advantage.

Low Impact, High Maintenance

If there is even the vaguest hint you are a low impact, high maintenance author you will not get your book published. They are a commissioning editor's nightmare from hell. The book didn't come in as good as you hoped, it isn't selling, and yet the author is having major fits about everything you do, is constantly on the phone and has even written to your boss a couple of times.

This might seem a lot about you and not much about the project but, I promise you, these things count. I know plenty of commissioning editors who will let a half decent proposal go if they get a strong feeling of high maintenance about the author. Especially if the book doesn't have to be written by you (ie if they can find somebody low maintenance to write a similar book) – normally non-fiction of course.

Re-read your draft proposal and think about how you will come across.

The last thing to do before sending it all in

When you think you are ready to go, get somebody else to read it all.

This could be a friend or colleague – it has to be somebody you trust to be honest. You want them to tell you if they spot any mistakes, how you come across as a person and if it all reads well to them.

Then, when you've had all the feedback you can get, put it aside and then after a few weeks, read it all again yourself. It doesn't matter how sick you are of tweaking, improving and checking it. The final thing you need to do is read every single word. *You only get one chance – you need it to be right.*

6 Sending it in and following it up

How to make your submission, guard your idea and chase it up

So, you've crafted your perfect submission. You're delighted with it. Time to send it off. But do you send it by post or email? What do you include and who do you actually send it to? Before you whack off a generic email to every publisher and agent you can find, time for a bit of thought…

The aim here is to get the submission to the right person, in the right form, at the right time and in the right way. Anything you can do to speed up that process is helpful.

Golden rule

Send it how the publisher or agent asks you to.

If the editor or agent says in *The Writers' and Artists' Yearbook/ The Writer's Handbook* 'written submissions only' then for goodness sake, don't call them. If it says on that publishers website 'call or email in the first instance' then that's exactly what you should do. Whatever you do, don't just whack off a standard email and send it to 20 different publishers and agents addressed 'dear sir or madam' when a quick look at the website or the *Yearbook* would tell you how each prefers to be approached.

If your idea is even going to be considered, then the first step is to avoid annoying the person you are approaching. So it's got to be how they want it.

Ideally it should also be personal. Check the *Yearbook/Handbook* and/or the publisher's website to see if there is a name you can identify as the right person (be slightly wary however – editors move around faster than books are updated and websites upgraded). If there is a name, it's definitely worth phoning the publisher or agency to check that person is still there. If you can't find a name, it's definitely worth phoning the publisher or agent, or emailing a general contact address to see if you can find the name of the appropriate person. If you are going to do this, be able to specify the name of the list or imprint or specific area (eg mind, body, spirit or history), or even a particular author: 'Can you tell me the name of the editor who published John Williams' book *Castles of England*?' or 'Can you tell me which agent handles Jenny Smith' is going to help the receptionist more than 'Can you tell me who to send my book on William the Conqueror to?'. Don't be surprised if it proves hard to get a name though – the receptionist might be a temp, or the company so big that they just guess a person at random. Plus of course publishers sometimes go to strange lengths to hide their editors from the outside world...

It is worth persevering though: if your proposal reaches the right person, first time, it not only increases your chances of success but it also endears you ever so slightly to that person (especially if you also spell their name correctly).

Email, phone or post?

Supposing you've got a choice of email address, phone number and postal address and no preference is specified – which should you use? Well, if you are great on the phone, by all means go for it, but remember that you are trying to convince somebody to publish what you write, not what you say. Personally, I always prefer books to be proposed in writing – after all, what I'm buying is your ability to write something interesting and write it well. When a book is published and on the retailer's shelf, it will sell (or not) on the basis of how interesting the title, jacket copy and writing is to the browser. The author won't be there to tell you how fantastic it is, and what it's really about is…

This said, one successful author tells me that she always phones before sending anything in, on the grounds that first you can check that you aren't wasting your time (ie you can ask if the idea in principle is appropriate for that person), and secondly that your submission will be recognised when it arrives at the recipient's desk. The author in question is exceptionally personable and seems always to be able to say just the right thing, and I can imagine that this would work for her. However, if you're anything less than very persuasive and assured on the phone, don't do it. If you do decide to take this tack, don't forget that you also need to be very good at judging whether you're saying the right thing and adapting mid-sentence if the vibes you get are bad.

Whatever you do, don't ever leave a phone message for an editor and say 'My name is Dan and I have a book idea. Call me back on this number………'. They won't. Or at least if they do, it's a miracle.

Personally, I have little preference between email and post. If in doubt, you could try both. Email is more convenient as I don't have to lug it about with me, but it can drop off the edges. Plus I usually prefer to read printed matter so if it's come by post I don't have to print it out. Emails tend to either be responded to more quickly, or not at all – depending on the editor's inbox efficiency. Post might take longer but is less likely to get lost. However if you do submit by post, include an email address so the editor can respond by email.

How to set out your proposal/submission

1. Follow that publisher's guidelines if there are any.
2. Always type. You'd be surprised. No handwriting, not even covering letters. If you've written your actual manuscript longhand and want to send a couple of chapters, type them up first (on a computer) or get somebody else to do it for you.
3. Set it out well – any sample chapters should always be double line spaced. Ditto the synopsis. Number the pages. Your covering letter should be single spaced, and no more than a page long.
4. Imagine somebody trying to read what you are sending. Is it going to annoy them that all the pages are fastened together so tightly? (Yes.) Will the slippy folder cause it to slide onto the floor? (Maybe.) Simply presented, neatly fastened but not so that it can't be unfastened, no gimmicks. No ring binders. No staples.

Do you send your submission to one publisher/agent or several?

This is one of the few points where there seems to be a deep division of opinion. Generally, some publishers and all agents seem to prefer single submissions. Pick one, send, wait. The problem is that most authors simply hate this as you can wait an eternity for a response to a submission (well, years have been reported and I confess to at least six months once or twice when the emails slipped off the system). So, many authors advise new writers to send multiple submissions and to hell with it.

Here are some points you might want to consider before you decide:

Personally I am always very pleased if an author says, 'you are my first choice publisher and I've only sent this to you, initially'. I like that. It puts me in a favourable frame of mind. But of course it doesn't guarantee the editor will get back to you quickly.

If a publisher says 'we're not interested in multiple submissions', then they might well really mean it. Think hard about whether you want to risk it. If they say no multiple submissions and you really want to go with them, then don't. You could put a deadline – 'if I don't hear back in a month then I will start approaching others – hope that's a reasonable time frame'. But you don't want to be too prescriptive.

However if I'm being really honest, I confess that if I know a book is sent to other publishers as well as me, then I may react quicker.

And finally, there's the fact that plenty of authors have sent multiple submissions and had their books published. Publishers may say they prefer single submission, but if the book is good enough, they are likely to waive that.

Agents are slightly different in that they only get paid if they sell your work, so the last thing they want to do is find they've invested time in a submission when you might well go with another agent. It's a slightly different scenario to publishers and I'd be more cautious about multiple agency submissions.

The worst situation from a publishing or agent perspective is not being sure. So, here's my advice:

1 Pick your genuine top publisher/agent. Write and tell them this and that you will hope to hear from them soon, and you'll hold off contacting anybody else for now. You can always send a follow up in a month or so and say really sorry not to have heard from you, will wait another couple of weeks and then sadly try elsewhere.

2 If you don't have a top publisher and are very desperate to get a response (do ask yourself why you are so desperate though) then send to all the appropriate ones *but be clear that's what you've done.*

Unconventional ways of getting to the right desk

We've assumed up to this point that you'll be making a cold approach. Needless to say, if there's any way you can warm up the approach, it's a very good idea. Do use your networks, investigate who knows who and hope that the six degrees of separation rule works and you can find a useful contact – either somebody in publishing who might be able to help, or a published author who could either act as your advocate or at least call in a favour and ask their editor to look at your proposal. Be warned though, big name authors are used to being badgered by those who would like to follow in their footsteps. They couldn't possibly help everybody. Occasionally though, a bit of guile can come in useful.

Case in point

Author Susan Hill got her big break when she wrote to Pamela Hansford Johnson, a well known novelist at the time, and asked for her advice. The reply suggested she keep writing and when she was ready, to write a book. When Susan completed her first book, she sent it to Hansford Johnson, who liked it, and recommended it to her publisher. The publisher liked it too, and thus Susan's first book was published, while she was still a teenager. Would this have happened without Hansford Johnson's priming the publisher? We'll never know but I'm sure at the very least it really helped.

SAE – essential or pointless?

Some publishers and agents explicitly ask for an SAE, in which case it pays to do as they ask. They will have their reasons. Just make sure it's big enough to hold whatever you sent, and it has sufficient postage attached.

However, if an SAE isn't specified, I wouldn't send one. Firstly, there's no point (do you really need the small number of dog eared pages back?) Secondly, some editors think it seems a bit defeatist.

Almost as if you are fully expecting them to hate it and as you have sent out so many, you really need to get it back so you can send it out again. And finally, I know I'm not the only editor who actually gets slightly peeved by the enclosure of an SAE. Why? Well, there are plenty of us who just don't return material, SAE or not. It seems pointless. If somebody has sent a small amount of material, as requested, then it's a hassle and not necessary as it won't be their only copy (it's done on a computer and saved on a computer). Easier and quicker just to put it in the recycling bin. If there's an intimation that I might do something unscrupulous with it (like give it to somebody else to read or copy or adapt) then I'd resent that. And to be honest if the editor is unscrupulous and wants to copy it, they could easily do that before returning it.

The only exception to this would be if you were sending a whole manuscript (when it has been requested) in which case I might enclose an SAE, but even then possibly not. Or if you send illustrations or some supporting material that was especially valuable – but in that case I'd send photocopies not originals.

Golden rule

Always keep a copy of everything you write. Never, ever send your only copy of anything to an agent or publisher. Back up computer files and save on at least one disk as well as on your hard drive. If it's your life's work, save on several disks and keep the copies in different places – maybe one even in a different building.

Illustrated books – do I send illustrations?

If you are proposing an illustrated book, whether for adults or children, then think very carefully before sending illustrations.

It's very tempting with children's books in particular, if it's for a young age group and there isn't much text, to send something, anything, rather than just send the words. Unless you are a very accomplished artist, and you want to send your submission on the basis of you being an author/illustrator, then don't send just anything. Better to send nothing at all than terrible sketches by your next door neighbour.

Remember that editors are used to commissioning illustrations from professional illustrators. They can visualise how you would illustrate a book without you having to spell it out for them. They will have a small group of freelancers whom they regularly use.

Following up

So, you sent your proposal in to a named person – agent or editor. And you waited, and you waited. And you waited. And now you can't bear it any more. So what do you do?

Here is a real email I received from a prospective author:

> Hi Rachael
>
> Really sorry for troubling you but I've been biting my nails the last couple of weeks and I'm almost down to my knuckles!
>
> I know you must have lots of these things to work through but just wondered if you have any headline feedback for me.

> Hope you don't mind me writing.
>
> All the best,
> Mark

How could this possibly annoy me? Despite the fact that I had towering piles of new proposals to look at, not to mention completed manuscripts to read, and was very stressed when I read it, this is human and real and very understanding. I didn't mind at all.

Contrast this with:

> Dear Rachael
>
> I sent you my book proposal two weeks' ago now and have heard nothing from you. Could you get back to me now, please?
>
> John

Insider's view

The commissioning editor sits at her desk. She's surrounded by piles of unread draft manuscripts and a few final ones. She's got a towering pile of proposals and an inbox so full that she is in trouble with IT. Your email arrives asking why she hasn't read your proposal yet. It's tetchy. Already under great pressure, her stress levels rise further. She looks at your proposal quickly and thinks 'It needs work, and I would do it if the author sounded good to work with but to be honest he sounds a bit high maintenance. No, better let it go.'

My advice generally would be this:

1 Never chase within two weeks at the very least, ideally a month. After that if you're going to do it, phrase your wording very carefully indeed.

2 Keep it simple. A short note is fine. Phoning every day or sending hugely long missives isn't. Remember the fine line between being a pest and persisting.

3 No two editors or agents are the same. Some will have very well organised systems and will always look at proposals promptly. Others (ahem) will try to be organised but will be a bit scatty and emails particularly can fall off the sides without them realising. A gentle note might be necessary.

4 Proposals will produce one of three reactions: immediate no, immediate yes or 'hmmm maybe I'd need to think about that.' You are likely to hear about the first two responses pretty quickly but the last is the one that might get delayed. If it's an 'immediate no' reaction and the reason is that your submission is so bad, or so inappropriate, you may just not hear back at all of course.

5 If the proposal is one the editor or agent wants to think about, unless you are absolutely desperate, let them think. If you push a person for an answer, it's likely to go the wrong way. As a commissioning editor I once knew said "If you want an answer right now, then it's no."

6 Whatever you do, don't lie about having offers on the table from other publishers. They may find out you're bluffing and it really won't go down well if you do.

7 If you genuinely have other publishers/agents interested, then be honest. That's one good reason to contact somebody and ask if they have had a chance to look at what you sent.

Case in point

I was once told by a prospective author that he needed an answer, as he had several offers. He asked for a ballpark of what advance and royalty we would offer, which I told him, and he said that was low on advance but above average on royalty, indicating he'd got financial packages sorted from others. I later reflected on the proposal and decided it wasn't right for me and advised him of this and that he would be better with one of his other offers who obviously were keen on the project 'as was'. Suddenly he was desperate to persuade me to stay with him and I began to suspect the other offers never actually existed. I became significantly less keen to work with him.

Ten dos and don'ts for sending in your submission

1 Do address your submission to a real person, by name, spelt correctly.

2 Do read the submission guidelines for that publisher or agent if they have them. Follow them to the letter.

3 Do set everything out clearly and make it easy to read. Double space and paginate sample chapters. Print on one side of the paper only.

4 Do include all your contact details: address, phone, email. Make it easy for them to get back to you in the way they prefer – not the way you prefer.

5 Do enclose an SAE if the agent or editor asks for one. Otherwise don't unless you desperately want it back for a legitimate reason.

6 Do always make sure there is sufficient postage on your package to cover what you send. A proposal that arrives with a demand for excess postage will not be looked favourably upon.

7 Don't try to make a publisher or agent feel sorry for you and take your submission because of that. They won't.

8 Don't include challenging statements like 'Are you the publisher with the vision to take this book on?' or 'Will you be the winner in the race to sign me up?'

9 Don't be arrogant. Be confident and assured, but not aggressive or superior.

10 Don't make demands. Be cheerful and optimistic, but not needy.

Protecting your idea – copyright, trademarks, confidentiality and non-disclosure agreements

So, you're ready to send off your submission to a publisher. Suddenly, a nagging doubt creeps in. How do I know that the publisher won't steal my idea? What if I send this off to them, and they pinch the essence of my book or plot and ask somebody they already know to write the same book? Uncomfortable thoughts. So what do you do?

The simple truth is that you don't know that any one publisher won't steal your idea. It's possible but highly unlikely. Most editors thankfully do have a sense of just and moral behaviour. Even the few who aren't so ethical know that publishing is a small world and you can find your name is mud extremely quickly.

However, I can't say it doesn't happen. I have come across authors who have sent an outline to a publisher, had it rejected or unacknowledged, and then discovered later that the same publisher has contracted one of their existing authors to write exactly the same book, with uncannily similar descriptive copy. This may be coincidence. It may not.

Is there anything you can do to protect yourself? Yes, there is. There are also things I really wouldn't advise. Here's a quick rundown of the good and the inadvisable ways to look after your intellectual property.

Confidentiality agreements/non-disclosure agreements

Every now and then, a commissioning editor gets a call or email from a prospective author saying 'I've got a book proposal for you, but before I show it you, I want you to sign a confidentiality agreement.' Not a terribly good idea. Most editors would just say no. Maybe all. I've never come across anybody who would sign one. The main reason is that truly original ideas are very, very rare. You'd be staggered how often a publisher receives two uncannily similar submissions in a week. Or how often a submission will come in with exactly the same approach to a subject that you've been discussing with another person just a few days beforehand. Imagine if as an editor you signed that agreement and then found to your horror the idea sent through was extremely close to one you were already in advanced discussions over?

Another reason that it's not a good idea to try and press an agreement on a publisher is that it smacks very strongly of 'high maintenance'. The editor will immediately have you marked as somebody who will be hard work, suspicious and could be a tricky customer to deal with. And taking it down to the personal basics, you are saying to the publisher that you mistrust them from the outset. Not really the kind of relationship you want to start.

Legal statements in covering letters

I'd avoid these for exactly the same reasons as above. A publisher will be instantly very wary of you and will probably steer clear.

Trademarks and copyright notices

I certainly wouldn't go overboard, but a little copyright line at the foot of each page that simply says ©Your Name, 2006 always seems a fair idea. It's subtle, but it's saying to the publisher 'I am aware of intellectual property, and I want to ensure my ideas are treated appropriately'. Anything you write is your copyright the minute you write it down (or record it another way), and doing this doesn't give you extra protection, but it's a simple reminder that won't go amiss.

You should be aware however that although a piece of writing has automatic copyright attached, there are some elements of a submission that don't carry any copyright. These include:

- Book titles
- Ideas

- The very basics of a plot
- Facts

Whether it's on a proposal or on the jacket of a published volume, there is no copyright in a book title. This means that in principle, you could write a novel called *Captain Corelli's Mandolin.* You would probably face legal action fairly swiftly, however, as there is a law against 'passing off' which means you can't give a book a title that means that it is pretending to be another well known book. Passing off applies only to published book titles, so whatever you call your book in proposal or submission form, it's difficult to protect.

What you can do is use a ™ notation alongside any 'brand' names in your proposal. For example, if you want to propose an exercise book based on a new method you have developed and called Tonacise, then it's probably worth using a capital T for Tonacise and a small ™ notation near the word.

Other ways to give yourself a little more protection include mentioning in your covering letter/email that this is your idea and you are sending it in confidence for consideration by the named editor (if possible).

Sending a copy of your submission

Some people advise sending an exact copy of your submission to your solicitor on the day you send it to the publisher, or to yourself by registered post, and keeping it unopened on arrival. The thought behind it is that if a publisher tries to steal your idea, you have evidence of what you sent and when. Personally I see little point, and wouldn't do it myself. Here's why.

If you've sent in a good idea, it's clear you can write and you are appropriately qualified to write it, then why wouldn't a publisher ask you to write it? The most healthy way of looking at the possibility of a publisher or agent pinching your idea is this: ask yourself why somebody might want to take the idea to another person, and then address any issues that spring to mind in your submission.

Here are some possible reasons you might come up with:

1 The idea is good but you aren't a 'name' in the field

In this case, why not mention in your proposal that if your not having a high profile is seen as an issue, then the following 'names' could be approached to provide a Foreword. Say if you would be willing to have a co-author who is a name.

2 The idea is good but you need a qualified person to write the book

If you do have qualifications or experience to support you as the potential author, make sure they are very well expressed and prominent. If you know you are lacking qualifications, again suggest in your proposal who might be approached for a Foreword, or to act as a consultant/advisor to the book, or to approach as a co-author. For example, if your book proposal is about healthy eating for kids, a child nutritionist or dietician could be useful to mention as an option.

3 The idea is good but you can't write well enough

This is possibly the most difficult one. If you know you are an expert in your subject but your writing isn't fluid or accomplished or of the right style, then address this up front. I don't think there's anything wrong with saying in a submission 'I have all the research to write the most incisive and riveting book about the French Resistance in WWII ever written. I am very happy to be coached in writing style or, if thought appropriate, to have a co-author or ghost writer, or to work closely with a hands on editor.' It sends out all the right messages to the publisher – I am flexible, open and willing to work with you. It does have implications however about cost to the publisher – or cost to you.

Finally, you need to accept that very few ideas are completely original. There is the possibility that a publisher might have received two very similar proposals close together. Sometimes it's spooky. But it does happen.

7 Negotiating a contract

How to get a handle on the basics and get a good deal

It's that moment every would-be author dreams about. The phone rings or the email pings and it's your editor or agent. You've been offered a contract.

Yes!

You've done it. Your book has been accepted. You're going to be published.

Before you know it your joy/relief (delete as applicable) is shattered as one of the following happens:

If you have an agent

Suddenly you realise that the agent is telling you that the publisher has offered this royalty and that advance and really it's not very satisfactory and they definitely want you to hold out for a better cut on the subrights and there's no way you should include US rights for this and what's more the other publisher who is interested is due to come back with an offer also but they haven't yet and the publisher who has offered wants an instant response…

If you are dealing direct with the publisher

You suddenly realise you're being offered this advance and that royalty rate, and do you want copyright assignment or exclusive licence in all media and languages, and for this level of discount only this royalty will apply, and on it goes... What's worse, in front of you is a 20 page document of impenetrable legalese that you're being asked to sign.

Help! Is this normal or are you being ripped off? Are you signing up for a nice income and good treatment or selling your soul to Lucifer? And what does it all actually mean anyway?

If you have a good agent, this is clearly where they come into their own and really add value. However, even when you have an agent it's useful at least to be able to understand enough to discuss what's on the table. If you are dealing direct with the publisher then you definitely need to have a good grasp of the key elements of the contract – even if just for peace of mind.

In this chapter we will have a quick run through the key elements of the deal making process and how it works, and then we'll gently walk through the key clauses in a contract. Of course, there are plenty of pointers as to where to go and seek help if you are really bewildered. There's nothing to fear. Honestly.

First things first.

A really core principle is: never, ever be afraid to ask what something means. If a publisher won't tell you in words you understand, then ask again. A good publisher will always be able and willing to explain the financial terms and contract clauses to you.

> **Insider's view**
>
> Negotiating contracts is never the favourite part of an editor's job. They do it because it's necessary, but frankly they want it to be as quick and painless as possible. Don't ask for changes for the sake of it – however, if there's anything you don't understand, even if it's tiresome for the editor to explain, it is part of their job and you as the author have every right to ask them to talk you through it.

The second core principle is: if you are going to negotiate, be nice but quietly determined and always look for a win-win. As with any kind of negotiation, if you can reach a point where both parties think they have won, it's the best kind of outcome you could possibly have.

The third core principle is: where there are lots of variables, decide which you care about and which you are less worried about so you can give on others but stick on some.

The smartest and most inspired author negotiation tactic along these lines that I have ever had came from Richard Craze.

"Quick, good, cheap.

You can have any two out of three."

This is so difficult to argue against. It seems the most reasonable thing in the world – and of course any editor will want all three and is completely floored by having to choose. Rich says that never yet has an editor said 'why can't I have all three?' I guess that's because it's brilliant logic to make you choose two. It's obvious that of the three, 'good' is a non-negotiable (for decent publishers at least) and therefore the editor is immediately on the back foot trying to decide whether to ask for 'cheap' or 'quick' – ie, increase the advance and royalty or accept a later deadline.

Oh and by the way, Rich says if you want to try this tactic, and you end up with more cash as a result, donations for the coaching tip are gratefully received.

Golden rule

Contracts work both ways. They are there to set out the obligations and responsibilities of both author and publisher. A good contract will protect you as well as protecting the publisher.

A word of reassurance

Like most people, you may be quite nervous about signing something legal. It's extremely unlikely that a reputable publisher will offer you something to sign that will later cause you extreme distress. It would be completely counterproductive; in a small community, where word gets around fast, soon nobody would want to publish with anybody who tried to cheat an author. Publishers tend to want happy authors. This is one of the main reasons I would always advise you to choose your publisher carefully. If they have lots of happy authors, it's a good sign. However, it's also fair to say that there are variables and that you're well advised to know what they are, so that you can get the best possible deal for yourself.

Negotiation of terms – what's fixed and what's not

Let's start with the most important bit for most people – the money.

Advance and Royalties

This is usually the central part of the contract offer. It determines how much money you are given up front and how much you earn per copy of the book sold. The first thing to remember is that an advance is exactly that – an advance on royalty. At this point you might want a quick refresher from Chapter 2 on how publishing works.

The publisher will normally make an offer. So for example, they might say they can offer you an advance of £4,000, split half on signature of the contract and half on delivery and acceptance of the manuscript. The royalties they are offering are 10% of net receipts (or 7.5% of published price).

At which point, the question is what do you say? How do you know if this is a good deal? And most importantly here, have they started low expecting you to negotiate, or are they offering perfectly standard terms and there is no room for manoeuvre?

This is actually quite tricky, as all publishers are a little different. It depends on the company and the individual concerned. For me as a publisher, it also depends who I am dealing with. So, for example, if it's an author I know well, I will know their individual circumstances and what's important to them and they will know that I'll give them a top or close to top offer and that it will be fair and equitable (as I'm that kind of person).

However, we'll assume here that this is your first book and you don't know the editor very well, and equally they don't know too much about you. We'll also assume you haven't discussed the financials at this point.

I will probably get into huge amounts of trouble for saying this, but as an author in these circumstances you have to assume there might be a bit of give in the offer. Normally, if everything isn't negotiable, then at least some of the components will be.

Before you make a response, think carefully about what's important to you. Is it how much you get up front? Or is it the longer term income? Do you want to publish with this company no matter what, or will you sell to the highest bidder? Are you willing to risk pushing so hard that you reach stalemate? And how important is the individual editor to you? All these factors influence how you tackle this.

If you are pleased with the offer, you like the publisher, and the money is only part of the equation, then you might want either to accept, or perhaps just to ask for a little bit of give on either the advance or the royalty rate.

If you feel you want more, then here are your options and how to go about it.

1 Go for a bigger advance

Some publishers don't compete on advances above a certain level, because it is a very risky business. Once you've paid out, unless your sales expectations are met, you can lose a lot of money. Others expect to compete on advances. The more you know about the publisher the more you are in a position of strength here. If advance is important to you, you can either choose to state a figure, or to express dissatisfaction and let the publisher respond with an improvement or another suggestion.

Good wording might be: 'I'm very pleased to get your offer and would really like you to publish my book, but I just wonder if you could improve the offer on the advance as it seems low.'

You could also, if you are brave, ask how that compares to the royalty that another author got (choose somebody comparable who the same company published not too long ago). It's a fair question.

Remember that the reason publishers are nervous about advances is the risk that is attached to them. Like the costs of editing, producing and printing the book, the advance is up front investment and may never be recouped. The publisher is putting their confidence – and their cash – in you and your book. If there's anything you can do at this stage to give the publisher more confidence (and reassurance), it should help you in your negotiations. So, if you can guarantee a bulk sale of the book once it's published, either to you or to a company or anybody, this will improve your chances of a bigger advance. If you can guarantee PR or marketing or get advertising for the book through contacts – the more you can bring to the table yourself, the more confident the publisher will be in increasing your advance.

A good publisher will always take into account what situation you are in. So, for example, if you are being offered a contract to write a popular history book and you need to invest substantial amounts of time to research the book, you will probably need the advance to live off for a while and a publisher should expect to give more up front. Similarly if you are a journalist, then writing a book means you're not earning any features income for a while so you might reasonable ask for a bigger than usual advance. However, if you are writing in your spare time, whilst working, or have finished the manuscript, then perhaps the editor might think that the advance isn't vital and therefore an average advance should be fine.

If you ask for a bigger advance and the publisher says they can't really go any higher, then obviously you have to make a judgement call based on what you know of the person, as to whether they are telling you the truth. If you think they are being up front, then you have to decide how important it is to you, or if it makes more sense to try and increase the royalty rate instead.

2 Ask for an improved royalty rate

There's lots of leeway here. You can ask for a higher starting rate, or a rising royalty depending on number of copies sold (if this hasn't already been offered, I would always ask for rising royalties). If a rising scale has been offered, you can ask for the number of copies at which the higher rate kicks in to be reduced, or for an additional royalty rate to be added on top of the current scale.

So for example:

If the offer is 10% of net receipts rising to 12.5% after 20,000 sales, you could suggest one of the following:

- 10% of NR rising to 12.5% after 10,000 sales
- 10% of NR rising to 12.5% after 15,000 sales and rising again to 15% after 30,000 sales

- 12.5% of NR rising to 15% after 30,000 sales

...and so on.

A good tip is to say 'I'm a little disappointed with the advance, but if the royalties could be improved to compensate, I can live with the advance.'

Generally publishers have a policy of paying either on net receipts or on the recommended retail price (the price on the jacket). There's usually not much point asking a publisher that pays on net receipts to pay you on retail price as it will be hell for them to administer. As long as the royalty rates are appropriate (10% or more on net receipts or 7.5% or more on retail price) then it shouldn't really matter.

Most of the discussion you will have will be about the standard royalty rates, but if your royalties are on net receipts there will be some other clauses in the contract to look out for.

High discount royalty

Most contracts have a clause that says for copies sold above a certain discount, the rate is a different one from the standard. This is often negotiable. Publishers may have a default figure that is automatically suggested in the contract, but which is lower than they will actually be willing to pay. The publishing argument is that if they are selling at a very high discount, the author should take part of the reduction in income. You could argue that if the royalty is on net receipts, you'll be getting a set percentage of less in any case, so what's the problem? If it were me negotiating the contract as an author, I wouldn't object if the high discount rate was a flat rate (ie the rising royalty scale didn't apply), as I can see that if a high royalty rate applies when the margins are very slim, it could be a killer for the publisher and maybe put them off including my book in a promotion. However, as an author I would ask if the flat rate could be the same as the regular edition starting royalty (10% net receipts, say).

Check what the high discount definition is and ask the publisher if any of their main retail clients get more than this as standard discount. Sometimes the discount level is negotiable. For example, if that publishers definition of high discount is 45% off retail price, you can be sure that some of the big booksellers are likely to get this as standard, and therefore some 'normal' sales will qualify for the lower royalty. There's a good case to be made that high discount should be set above the rate of normal terms with most retailers.

Bookclub royalties

This is similar to high discount royalties. Book clubs place very large and firm orders (ie the copies can't be returned) but in return they insist on extremely high discount. You may be asked to take a lower royalty to make this work financially. Though it's always worth asking for this to be increased if money is your prime objective, if a publisher tells you that to give you more than you are asking means the deal is unlikely to be viable, and they seem genuine, then it's worth thinking about whether you are (a) shooting yourself in the foot by making it impossible for the publisher to make a deal profitable for them by your demands and/or (b) if you are annoying the editor and causing extra aggravation for all of you for something that might or might not happen. It is a guaranteed sale after all, and the volume of the sale normally makes up for the cut in royalty.

Copyright or exclusive licence

There are three kinds of contract you might be offered in respect of copyright:

1 **Exclusive licence**

This is when you retain copyright in the book, but grant the publisher exclusive licence to exploit it, usually in all media, all languages, all territories (we'll look at this separate issue of what rights you grant the publisher below).

2 **Copyright assignment**

In this kind of contract, you assign copyright in the book to the publisher. They then become the copyright holder for the time the contract is in place (note: not automatically forever).

3 **You sign over all rights**

This is very rare, and really only applies to a small proportion of contracts with highly illustrated publishers. If you've agreed to do a writing job, for a flat fee, for a highly illustrated publisher or packager, they may ask you to sign all rights over to them – ie you don't hold copyright, nor do you grant an exclusive licence, instead you sign away any and all rights you have in connection with the words. They are effectively 'buying in a bit of writing' in the way they may buy in illustrations. You should only ever agree to this if the book is the publisher's idea, not yours, and if you are happy with that arrangement. Full time writers often accept it as they are effectively being commissioned to write a set number of words and are OK in having no rights over what happens to it in the future.

So the vast majority of contracts will be either the first or second type. Two very important points apply to these two:

1 If you assign copyright to the publisher, it is only for the duration of the contract. If the contract is terminated, all rights revert to you. The contract can terminate for several reasons – they are set out in the contract and you should note them carefully. The most important one to check for is that if the book goes out of print, the contract should terminate, and all rights should revert to you.

2 Although to many authors it feels instinctively quite important to retain copyright, it's worth knowing that most big publishers are careful to make sure there's not really an awful lot of difference between the two in practical terms. It's very unlikely that you will be able to do anything with your material under an exclusive licence contract that you couldn't under a copyright assignment. So much so in fact that the main difference is usually that under copyright assignment, your name is next to the little © on the title verso page, whereas under an exclusive licence agreement it would be the publisher's name.

The reason publishers generally say they prefer copyright to be theirs is that they can defend any breach of that copyright more effectively. And they will stand the cost of doing so. Under an exclusive licence agreement, you as copyright holder are (in theory at least) jointly liable for defending any breach.

Either way, you will usually be expected to sign an agreement for 'the full period of copyright' which is your life plus 70 years. This is usual and publishers normally would strongly resist any attempt to put a set time on the agreement. There's not much point in trying to limit the agreement to a set number of years, though you can try if you feel strongly about it. Personally I wouldn't worry, as if the publisher breaches the contract then all rights revert to you anyway.

It's your call. If it worries you not to keep copyright, ask for exclusive licence.

Golden rule

A good contract will ensure that if a book goes out of print, all rights revert to you.

All rights and languages

Normally a publisher wants all rights and languages in your book – this will be assumed unless you specify otherwise. If you are worried about the publisher's ability to exploit as many rights and languages as possible, you could stipulate that you wanted to retain the rights to certain media or languages. For example, if you have checked and you know that the publisher in question has no US division and has had no success in selling US rights for any of its books, you might ask that you retain US rights.

Additionally, you may believe that you should keep certain rights, such as TV or merchandising rights. If you do want this, you must get it written into the contract. There are cases where authors realised too late what they had inadvertently signed away.

Golden rule

Think very hard about what rights you think the publisher should have and what you want to keep.

If the book is your idea, and if for example you have already worked to establish a brand of which the book is a part, you might want to ensure you hand over only book rights, and that TV, merchandising etc are clearly excluded. On the other hand, if the book is the publisher's idea, it's probably fair that they have first option on exploiting all rights.

The two things always to bear in mind are:

1. Was it my idea or the publisher's?
2. Is this likely to be significant with this book or am I arguing over nothing?

If you have an agent, they may want to try and keep as many rights as possible, so they can sell them themselves. It makes sense if you are an agent and are confident you can sell a fair number of rights: if the publisher sells the rights, they take a split. If the agent sells the rights, the publisher is cut from the equation and you (and therefore the agent) get more from each deal.

However. Most publishers will want to sell the rights themselves (especially foreign language) – they see it is part of the overall picture on generating income from the book and believe that as they are taking all the financial risk, it's fair that they are getting a return from this.

As a rule, I would say that if you don't have an agent, and usually even if you do, if the publisher wants to try and exploit all language and territory rights, and has a reasonable chance of doing so (either by track record or by convincing you something has happened to mean they can do it) then it's probably fair to let them go ahead. What I would consider however, is asking whether any unsold rights can be reverted to you after a certain time has passed, if you ask for them to be reverted. So, for example, if after two years they have not sold the US rights (or Polish, or Romanian, or whatever) then you can ask for these rights back and try to sell them yourself. I would say that's a fair deal and as a publisher I never have any objection to this. If the publisher has a reasonable time frame to achieve the sale, they can't complain if you as the author want to have a go. Two years is reasonable. They may agree to 18 months – or even a year. It all depends how much it means to you, and how likely you think you are to succeed.

Two final points on the issue of rights:

1 Authors often assume that if a company is large and has a division in the US and one in the UK, for example, that signing a deal with the UK side of the company will automatically mean their book will go to the US also. Not the case. It may happen as a matter of course, but more likely the US division will be independent and the US editors or salespeople decide whether or not they want a particular book. If in doubt about how the publisher you're talking to works, ask.

2 If a publisher is large and has offices in several countries, they are likely to offer first option in a language to their own office in that territory. That might not mean they get the best financial deal.

Publishers make the case that keeping the foreign language editions 'in the family' where possible brings additional benefits in sharing marketing material, promotional strategies and enabling joined up thinking internationally. Hence it's about more than just selling to the highest bidder.

Subrights royalties

Your contract will probably refer to subrights royalties, when referring to a situation as outlined above where they license another publisher (or other company) to exploit specific rights in the book. For example, a deal with a Russian publisher to produce a Russian language edition of the book. Or the audio rights to produce an audio CD of the book. The way these work financially is that the Russian publisher (say) pays the publisher an advance and royalty for the right to translate and publish the book, and the publisher then splits this income with you.

In the contract it states what percentage of the income from such deals you get, and what percentage the publisher gets. Now, here's where we enter a tricky field, because the split varies so widely according to type of book, type of publisher, set-up of publisher, other factors on the table, how much the publisher wants your book, and so much more. I can't give you an average. You might get anything between a 50/50 split between you and the publisher up to an 80/20 split in your favour. The former would be more likely on textbooks and the latter for fiction with a good agent.

Publishers argue that a lot of work goes into selling rights (which it undoubtedly does – Frankfurt Book Fair is just the highlight of a year round sales job by rights professionals). As a result they want what they see as a fair cut of this income. Whether you want to argue to the death about an extra 5-10% or so is up to you. As always, my advice would be to measure the potential gain and the potential aggravation when deciding how much to push on these kinds of things.

Generally, I think it's fair to say that the subrights royalty split is a point that authors don't tend to worry too much about, but agents are very focused on.

Insider's view

Most authors are absolutely delighted when they learn that their book is to be translated into any language – after all, it's fantastic to know that what you wrote will soon be read by people in Lithuania or China. And having copies of your book in Chinese on your shelf is a talking point (and not much use otherwise...).

However, one non-fiction author got very upset when he discovered that he had no control over the financial terms agreed by his publisher with foreign language publishers. He hadn't realised that he wouldn't be consulted over what advance and royalty was accepted for each language. Of course this is an issue only if your book happens to be incredibly successful (otherwise you'd be like the authors above and just delighted it's happening at all). It is up to the publisher to negotiate terms if they are exploiting the rights, and it's worth knowing this. If you have strong feelings about this issue – as with any – tell your publisher in advance.

Warranties and indemnities

These clauses are usually set in stone. I don't know any publishers who will remove these, as to do so means that their insurers don't cover them if they get sued for libel or breach of copyright etc. What the warranties and indemnities usually do is to get you to say by signing the contract that all the work you provide is original and your own work and that it has not been copied from anybody else's work. It also says that you have said nothing in your work that is libellous, malicious, or could cause any injury to another, and so on. What this means is that if somebody comes along and accuses you of plagiarism, for example, by claiming that one chapter of your book is copied from a chapter of their book, you as the author are completely liable for any costs. This is fair enough, if that's what you did of course.

What a few authors have a problem with (and more than a few agents) is if the warranties and indemnities include alleged breaches as well as proven ones. So in this case if somebody alleges that you copied their work, you would be liable for defending this allegation in court (if it came to that). In practice, your publisher might be willing to defend this for you, as if the allegation was proved to be false then the accuser should foot any legal bill, and if it were proven, then you'd foot the bill anyway. You can't count on it, as I'm sure not all publishers would. There may well be no negotiation on this, as your publisher may say that the contract has to include alleged breach for their indemnity insurance to be valid.

Personally, if I were signing a contract as an author (as in fact I have done for this book of course) I wouldn't worry about this. Most publishers are firm on the point and there is little room for negotiation. You can try of course, but your best course of action is to be scrupulously careful to avoid plagiarism, libel or anything that might land you in trouble.

Competing works

There will often be a clause that prevents you from writing a competing work for another publisher. I would ask for this to be as specific as possible – ideally to define a competing work as 'a book on exactly the same subject at exactly the same level' or similar.

Don't ever sign away your right to write any other book on the same subject. Especially if you are a specialist in an area.

Deadline

A deadline for delivery is usually a component of the contract. This may be imposed by the publisher due to their commitments, or you might be asked to suggest a deadline. The first thing to do before agreeing a deadline is to ask how vital it is that you meet whatever date is agreed. As discussed in Chapter 8 on working with your publisher, for some publishers it's absolutely critical, for others it can be a moveable feast. Usually it's very important you meet the date, so I would err very much on the side of caution when agreeing a date and try to build in at least two or three weeks more than you think you can possibly need. Most authors find it takes longer than anticipated to finish a book to their satisfaction. Writing can be tiring and you need frequent breaks. Some days you might write 3,000 words – other days you might struggle to produce much of value at all. If you don't have a clue, assume that you can write say 1,500 words a day, but don't expect to work every day at this rate.

Above all, you know yourself. Be honest about what you can achieve.

Always remember that a contract will give the publisher the right to decline to publish the book if you are late in delivering. They might not take this option, but then again, they might…

Electronic rights

As electronic rights (for example to produce an e-book – a downloadable version of the book) are relatively recent, there aren't the same standard terms as for print copies. Publishers are on the whole still trying to work out how to make e-books pay. They are cheap to produce, but only if you have already put the investment in to the editing, typesetting, etc for the print copy. They are high revenue to sell, as usually there is no retailer involved, but only if you can reach the customer direct. They are very portable, but only if you have sufficiently good hardware that you can bear to read the book on screen. As you can see, there are a lot of 'but' factors. Some people believe that electronic rights will become terribly important, when advances in hardware make it as easy and comfortable to read a book off screen as in paper form. However, until that time (which will be when? anybody's guess) it's unlikely to be a significant source of income – if indeed any electronic rights are exploited at all.

As you can see, with so much hanging in the air it's hard for anybody to know what a fair royalty on an electronic version is or will be. Some argue you should get the same as a print copy or more, others say it should be the same or less (usually agents and author go for the former and publishers the latter, oddly enough). The worrying aspect is what might happen in the future technologically, leaving you tied to inappropriate terms. To avoid this, some publishers are now willing to add a clause saying that if at some point in the future the rate seems inappropriate, you can ask for it to be reviewed by the publisher and, if still not happy, by an independent arbitrator. This is a good idea.

Accounting

Ensure the contract says how many times a year the accounts are done and the author receives a statement (and is paid). It's normally between once and three times, with twice being most common.

Permissions

If you quote from another book, or use anybody else's material in your book, then you may need to seek permission to do so. Just as others will have to ask you for permission if they want to use anything you have written. If you use a small amount of material (up to 75 words) then that *should* be covered by the 'fair usage' principle, *so long as* you fully credit the source of the material. To use substantial amounts of somebody else's material while it is still in copyright (life of the author plus 70 years) means either you or the publisher must ask for permission, and pay the requested fee if appropriate.

Golden rule

If in doubt ask for permission. Or don't use the material.

Some sources of material are more tricky than others – it's very unlikely anybody will object to you quoting a line from a book so long as you credit the author and source. However, film studios are notoriously funny about allowing people to quote from films, and song lyrics can be fiercely protected too.

Normally the contract states who is expected to apply for any necessary permissions, and equally who pays for any clearance fees. Make sure you are happy with this and, if it's you, that you know what's involved. Permissions is a complex area and can be a minefield. If at all possible, ask that the publisher clears permissions or at least highlights what will need permission clearing. If you ask the publisher to agree to cover any permission fees, they will almost certainly want to put a limit on the amount they are willing to pay for this – and are likely to put this in the contract. If you go over the amount, the excess is likely to be deducted from your royalties.

If you are asked to apply for permissions yourself, ask the publisher to provide you with a letter that you can use. This will ensure you use the right wording. Be aware it could be expensive and if in doubt, ask the publisher if they will give you something towards the cost of permissions.

New editions

The contract should stipulate whether it covers revised editions of the book and what happens to royalties for any new edition (sometimes they are set to return to the base level of a rising royalty). Are you happy with this? If not, you can ask to change the contract so that perhaps royalties go back one stage, temporarily, and then continue to rise. Alternatively you may want to ask that the contract state that new edition terms will be renegotiated at the time.

The reason publishers sometimes stipulate that royalties will revert to the original starting royalty for a new edition, is that new editions involve reinvesting in the book (new typesetting, editing, jacket design etc). They want to recoup the new investment from book sales before you start escalating up a royalty scale again.

The contract may say that if you are asked to do a revision of the book, but are not willing or able to, the publisher can pay somebody else to do this instead. The amount may be deducted from your royalties. Now is the time to talk to your publisher about this if you don't like it.

Multiple book contracts

In fiction especially, it's fairly common for a new author to be contracted for more than one book. This is primarily because fiction publishers know that sometimes a first novel does reasonably well for a new author, but it's the second book that hits the big time. It's also because if a publisher is taking a big risk on the author, should it pay off they want to know their return on investment is being maximised. It's also security for the author – you know your next book will be published, whatever happens to the first.

Option on future books

If your contract is for one book only, the publisher may try to include a clause stating that they have first option on your next book. It's up to you whether or not this is acceptable. You may feel that the publisher should earn the right to publish your next book. It's much more common in fiction to have multiple book deals, or for there to be an option on your next book. In non-fiction, it's reasonable to ask the publisher to remove this obligation and let the publisher know that if they do a good job, they will get your next book.

Termination of contract

All contracts will outline under what conditions the contract terminates, and if copyright and all other rights revert to you, the author, when it does. Check these carefully. Normally the publisher has a right to terminate the contract if the author doesn't deliver on time (so be careful what you agree on as a deadline – and meet it come hell or high water, unless you have agreed an extension in writing). They should also have the option to terminate the contract if what you deliver doesn't conform to the agreed scope and quality (again, agree as much as you can, as explicitly as you can on what you are writing). From your side, you should be able to terminate the contract if the publisher doesn't publish within a certain time after you deliver and they accept the manuscript (talk to your publisher about what time frame would be reasonable). The contract should terminate automatically if the book goes out of print, but you should also be able to ask for termination of contract if the book is out of stock for a significant period. (Out of stock means there are no copies in the publisher's warehouse, but they haven't officially said they won't be printing any more. Out of print means there has been a decision not to reprint.)

The arrival of print on demand (POD) has muddied the waters here a little – a publisher can say a book is not out of print even when they have no stock, if they have a print on demand programme. This means that books are digitally printed to order (as opposed to using a printing press), and this can be economically viable for just one copy at a time. If you don't want your book to be in the print on demand programme, for example if you want to see whether another publisher will take it on, then you should have the right to ask for the contract to terminate.

Golden rule

Always make sure you understand your obligations under the contract, and that you are happy with the publisher's obligations too.

Other clauses

I would always make sure the following clauses were in a contract:

- Something to say your moral rights are recognised as author of the work – this means that you will always be identified as the author, on all editions of your book. It also means that nobody can 'distort or mutilate' your work in a way that would damage your reputation.
- A clause or appendix to describe the scope and nature of the work (we'll come back to this in the next chapter). It will give you clarity over what you have both agreed you are writing, and protect you from having your manuscript being rejected on spurious grounds.

Where to get advice

If you don't have an agent, but you'd still like somebody with suitable qualifications to have a look at a contract for you, I would highly recommend joining the Society of Authors. They go through your contract clause by clause, tell you how the terms offered relate to industry standard and flag any clauses that cause them concern (and tell you why and what you might want to check with the publisher). For more details about what they offer see

www.societyofauthors.net. It costs £80 to join at the time of going to press (or £56 if you are under 35 and don't earn much from writing yet) – I'd say that gives great value for money if you feel concerned about negotiating a contract on your own. It's certainly cheaper than an agent, if you've got this far without one. They will also give you professional advice on any issue such as copyright, libel and so on.

You can't join the Society of Authors until you have an offer of a contract – but that's when most authors feel they need the advice. The exception to this is if you have either had a book published or self published for profit, or if you've had a dozen or more articles published or broadcast previously.

You may be thinking of asking a legal expert for advice. This can be expensive and far, far too cautious in the advice that is offered. I wouldn't personally recommend going to a lawyer for advice on a publishing contract unless there's something you are really concerned about for a particular reason. As a publisher, my experience is that negotiating contracts with authors advised by lawyers is like pulling teeth. Unless they really understand publishing very well (which most don't), it's unbelievably frustrating and may even leave your editor wanting to say 'just forget it – I can't take any more'. Which is not really a good thing. That's not to mention the expense.

However, I do know of published authors who use the services of a lawyer for contractual consultation, and have been very happy with it. I think that if it's going to work, you would probably already have a lawyer on some kind of retainer (so it doesn't cost you the earth) and you will filter the advice yourself before passing it on to weed out anything you think is excessively cautious or unnecessary.

One special circumstance I can think of where a lawyer might be worth considering would be to check the contract if you have a really big offer on the table, and have managed to get this far without an agent. A one-off lawyer's fee for overseeing the contract negotiations could work out better value (at least financially, this time) than paying an agent a percentage of all your receipts on that book indefinitely.

Interestingly, no two agents or authors (or lawyers even) ever have exactly the same concerns about a standard contract in my experience. Everybody has particular concerns relating to their previous experiences and their circumstances. One person will be desperately concerned about clauses that another author or agent won't even query. I would always suggest that you filter any advice you get from an external source, be it the Society of Authors or whoever, through your own personal logic check to see if the guidance makes sense to you. If you aren't worried about a particular element of the contract, don't feel you have to argue it. If it doesn't worry you in your circumstances for your particular book, that's usually a good reality check to let it stand and concentrate on anything you do have concerns about.

Further advice can also be obtained from more exhaustive books (see **www.whiteladderpress.com** for an up-to-date list). Michael Legat's book is widely regarded as the most thorough on the subject for authors. If you buy it, you'll see that we don't necessarily attach the same importance to the same clauses. Such is the nature of contracts. What one author (or publisher) sees as terribly important, another might not. Again, you be the judge as to whether it matters to you.

8 Working with your publisher

How to make sure it all goes smoothly after the contract is done

Congratulations! The hard bit is over. You've got a publishing deal, you've negotiated the contract and the ink is drying. Now what? You could argue that we've now reached the end point for this book. Not so fast. Firstly, your book isn't actually published yet – it's commissioned, but there's many a slip twixt contract and bound copy. Even if the writing goes well and your manuscript is accepted without condition, it's one thing having your book published, but it's another having it published so it's just the way you want it. And so that it goes on and sells as many copies as it possibly can.

The way you work with your publisher from here on will be critical in making your book as successful as possible.

One of the founders of a new independent publisher told me that the reason she and her partner started their business was because of her partner's dreadful experience in having his first book published. It was so bad, she said, that they started up their own enterprise to prove that publishing didn't have to be like that. In many ways, the relief of getting a contract can leave you rather vulnerable to things not turning out quite as you hoped thereafter. To make sure your experience isn't a bad one, this chapter will set out what to expect from here on, and what you can do to help your publisher (and, yes, keep them on their toes).

As soon as the contract is signed, ask your editor how they would like to work from here on. Here are the key things you might want to check up on:

1 What would your editor like to see, in what form and when?

On your contract you will have a deadline for the whole complete manuscript (assuming of course it's not already written). Does your editor not want to see anything until then? Or would they like to review chapters as they are completed? The editor should take into account how you'd prefer to work – but if they want to see chapters one at a time and you are dead set against them seeing anything more until it's done and dusted, you'll need to work something out between you.

2 Do you need any more discussion at this stage on the contents list/outline/sample material/sample chapters/subplot/characters? Or can they now be agreed on between you?

If you want to save yourself from nasty shocks down the line, and protect your book while you are at it, make sure you agree in writing on an outline, scope, style, contents and ideally a sample chapter. There are major reasons for this.

Firstly, you don't want to be in a position where you deliver your manuscript and it gets rejected for not being what the publisher wanted. Remember, a contract can be cancelled if the publisher rejects your manuscript for not conforming to quality, scope or extent. The more you can agree on at this early stage, the less room there is for misunderstanding between you about what you are writing and how. It also means that an unscrupulous or sloppy publisher will find it less easy to change their mind about what it is they want, and cause you extra work or cancel your contract unfairly. Plus it gives you extra guidance on what to write – useful in non-fiction especially, if structure and discipline aren't your strong points.

3 **Are you expected to keep records of permissions that need to be sought? Do you need to apply for them or will this be done by the publisher (or 'in house' as they call it) at a later date?**

   A good publisher should tell you how the process works from here on, but broadly speaking here's what to expect.

If you have already written the book (usually fiction)

Move on to the section headed *Manuscript Handover* below.

If you've not written the book yet

Your contract will state that you've agreed to deliver a manuscript of a certain length (normally in number of words, possibly in number of printed pages) of agreed subject, scope and quality, by a certain date. Assuming you write the book that you've agreed, then the most important thing is to meet that delivery date. Some publishers will have fixed the publication date eight or more months in advance, and slippage is bad news for them. All publishers struggle with this. As a first time author you have to be sure you deliver on time.

If you get half way into the book and realise it's not going to be possible to meet the date, discuss this with your editor as soon as possible. That way they can shift the publication date if possible, and will at least be forewarned. Some publishers (especially illustrated non-fiction) publish in two specific seasons – spring and autumn. A book slipping into January when they were expecting to publish in October is a disaster – not only is it missing the season, but it's out of the fiscal year probably too. And worse, if you are an illustrated publisher with co-editions, you will have contracts with your co-edition customers that bind you to delivering a particular book on a particular date. It's absolutely crucial to keep on track. Whatever you do, keep to time. Other publishers will be less bothered about the exact publication date, and will ask you to spend more time getting it right and not worry about the date. But even if you're lucky enough to be writing for such a publisher, keep them up to date with progress. They will appreciate your courtesy.

Every publisher has one – the Jurassic Park book. So named because it's been 10 million years in the making. Or it feels like it. You are really pushing your luck if you keep delaying handover, as most publishers will not be able to give you this kind of leeway. Here are just two reasons why:

1. They've probably already announced the book to the retailers. It annoys retailers to be told a book isn't publishing when they were told it was – particularly if they have plans for it.

2. Publishers are businesses and have projected revenue based on publication of your book at a set time. If it's late, it's a big issue – the smaller the publisher the more critical to business survival that is.

If you are very late, the publisher has the right to cancel your contract, or bring in somebody else to finish the book (not for fiction, clearly). You are safer if:

- You are especially valuable to the publisher
- They desperately want your book
- Nobody else could write that particular book

If the publisher took the idea to you, you are on very rocky ground. If it was your idea, you should have more say about them trying to bring in somebody else to finish the book off – check your contract carefully.

The easiest way to avoid angst is simply not to be late. Agree a realistic deadline from the outset. Build in leeway for slippage in writing. Be nice to your publisher. Don't be a dinosaur author.

What to do when you are ready to deliver

Golden rule

Ask the editor what they want. Please!

This applies however many books you have written. Do they want the manuscript in hard copy, electronic form or both initially? Don't forget to double space and paginate.

Before you send anything off, it really pays to get somebody else to read it. Whether you choose a friend, colleague, somebody who would be in your target market, or somebody who is thoughtful and logical, they may be able to pick up things you have missed. When you've worked solidly on a book for a long time, you can become too close to it and miss glaring errors or omissions.

Submitting the manuscript

On or about your deadline you should hand over your manuscript in exactly the form the publisher requests. Then you wait.

Golden rule

When you have sent the book in, don't panic if you don't hear anything back for a while. The editor is probably just busy and hasn't had a chance to look at it yet.

It's very easy to start getting carried away with doom scenarios if you don't hear back within 24 hours of submission. You start having visions of the editor with head in hands and red pen scrawling big thick lines through your precious work. It's far more likely that the book is sitting like a virgin on the pile high desk waiting for the editor to clear enough space out of the way even to start reading it.

Sometimes publishers forget just how nerve-wracking it is for authors to wait for the feedback. Manuscripts don't always come in exactly when you expect them to (though you delivered on time, there are plenty who don't) and editors can end up with a backlog. If you don't hear back, ask gently if they have any idea when it will be read, just so you know and can stop worrying. If your editor is human, that'll be fine.

Manuscript handover

The editor (or somebody else appointed by the editor) will then read your manuscript and then let you have feedback. At this stage it will be broad feedback: structure, voice, characterisation, flow, level of writing, etc. Sometimes this is known as a 'structural edit'. The nitty-gritty copyediting for typos, grammar and so on comes later.

You will then work with the editor to address any issues the editor has raised. Many of their points you will probably agree with, some you can discuss and reach an agreement. There may be points however, where you absolutely fundamentally disagree and obviously you then need to sit down with the editor and try to work through to an understanding, one way or the other. It's vital that you have a good relationship with the editor if this process is to work well, which is one of the reasons I believe that picking your publisher at least partly on the basis of which editor you 'gel' with the best, and how much you respect their opinion and ability, is a pretty good strategy.

In some types of non-fiction, particularly specialist publishing (scientific, technical and medical for example) the commissioning editor is unlikely to read every word. In fact they may not read very much at all. They may either accept it because you are the leading authority, or they may send it out for peer review. Be prepared for this. The book will always (or should always) be read word for word by the copy editor, if nobody else.

After feedback from the commissioning editor, you will be asked to revise the manuscript if necessary. When you resubmit, the editor should hopefully then accept your manuscript, at which point you will be paid any advance due on delivery and acceptance (note you won't necessarily receive the money straight away, it could be up to 30 days later).

Final manuscript handover to publication

It's now that the copy editor will read your manuscript, come back to you with any queries, and the text design (the design of the book interior) will be done. When the text is copyedited and the book design done, the text will be flowed into the design (known as typesetting), and you will then be sent page proofs. You should at this stage have the opportunity to read the whole book as laid out in pages, and to correct any errors. This is not the time to be rewriting the book – if you try and do so, you may be charged any excess correction costs. Most publishers are quite picky about this, as it is expensive to re-typeset because you suddenly decide that maybe you should rewrite three pages in Chapter 2.

At the same time as you are reading proofs, the publisher will pay a proofreader to read them also, and pick up any typos or missed errors or inconsistencies. Your corrections and those of the proofreader are then collated onto one set of page proofs, and these are sent back to the typesetter to be dealt with. A new set of proofs called revises are then produced. You may or may not see these, depending on the publisher. Most are terrified that you will suddenly decide to make more changes and opt for keeping you away from them. Really it shouldn't be necessary to see them as the revises are just to check that all changes have been properly made, and no new errors introduced.

The book then goes to press, and it's all over for you until the advance bound copies arrive in the post.

This description of the process makes it sound as if it all happens very quickly. It doesn't. Most authors are surprised just how long it takes to get from proposal to publication. It's likely to be somewhere between six months and a couple of years.

The jacket

The book cover, or jacket, can be the subject of some tension between author and publisher. You may have quite strong feelings about the jacket, or even specific ideas about how it should look, in which case you need to tell the publisher about this as early as possible – definitely before you hand your manuscript over. Most publishers prepare jackets six to eight months before the book is due to be published – possibly even earlier. This is because advance selling of your book will start about that time before publication, and the jacket is a vital part of the advance selling process. You can't underestimate the power of a jacket – apart from a bit of descriptive blurb in the sales kit, or Advance Information sheet (AI for short), the jacket is the representation of what they are buying.

The jacket is seen as the publisher's responsibility, and the publisher has the final say. It is viewed as part of the marketing, which it undoubtedly is. This may cause you some anxiety. I guess I would say this: generally, publishers do have a lot of experience in producing jackets that sell.

You should be shown the jacket design(s) when ready, if not for approval, then for information. Hopefully you like it and are relieved and excited. But what do you do if you really hate it? Firstly, reflect. Is it really that bad? Is it just not your taste or do you seriously think it will damage the book? If you are still worried, tell your editor how you feel and what exactly it is about the jacket you don't like. I would very much hope that your editor would at least hear you out. Hopefully a few tweaks will make both sides happy. If not, then the editor then has three choices – to change the jacket, to persuade you it's OK, or to insist on using the jacket as it is.

Usually, the contract stipulates that the publisher has final say over the jacket. However, the editor will clearly be weighing up the jacket itself and the relationship with you. What I sometimes do if there's a difference of opinion, is show the intended jacket to a bookbuyer for a key retail chain and ask them what they think. If a key buyer says they love it, then most authors would accept that as being a valid reason to keep it and put aside their initial personal preferences. It might be worth asking your editor if they will do this, if you ever get into a face-off situation.

What to do when...

Here are my bits of advice for a range of possible situations that might arise during the writing phase. Many of these are common worries for authors.

What to do if you get stuck

Writers block happens to everybody at some point. Don't panic. Pick up the phone and have a chat with your editor or agent. Talking over what you're stuck on may help, and your editor or agent will have been through the same experience with plenty of other authors.

The best bit of advice is probably to stop worrying about whether it's good enough and just keep writing. You can edit and rewrite your work later if necessary.

> "Don't get it right, get it written. Most of all, believe in yourself"
> *Carol Smith, agent turned writer*

What to do if somebody else publishes a very similar book while you are writing yours

It happens. And it's absolutely gutting when it does. You're midway through your manuscript and then you happen to be searching on amazon one day and horror of all horrors, you see a book about to publish that is almost exactly the same as yours in scope and market. All you can really do is get on with it, and work as hard as you can to make sure your book will be the best it can be. Your publisher should be understanding on this point. Work with them to explore how to make your book better or to reach the market more effectively. It needn't be the death knell for your book.

The final question when this happens is: 'should you read the competitor book while writing yours?' This is a tricky one and everybody is different. I know authors who will read everything they can find on a subject before they start writing. They call it research. Personally, I'm with the group that wouldn't actually read the competition just before writing my book. I'd want to know roughly what they covered, but I'd rather do it my own way, and avoid being influenced by others at that stage.

What to do if your editor moves on while you are writing

Your contract is with the publishing house, not with the editor. This may be a real blow to you, but that's the way it is. For this reason it's never a bad idea to see if you can engineer to meet your editor's boss at some point, just in case. (Not in a way that makes your editor think you think you are too big a fish to talk to them.) It's fairly common for big selling authors to move publisher to follow an editor they like, and you can always do this for your next book. For now, you just look to bond with your editor's successor as quickly as possible.

What to do if your publisher tries to cancel your contract before delivery

It's rare, but it does happen. The first thing you need to do is check your contract carefully. Particularly in highly illustrated publishing, because of the reliance on co-editions and publishing on time, you may have a clause that says that you are asked to deliver in batches, and that at any time the publisher can terminate the contract if you aren't delivering the required quality. This is so the publisher has time to find and recruit somebody else to finish the job if necessary. They should however always give you the chance to put right what is wrong before cancelling.

If you suspect a publisher is trying to cancel a contract because they have changed their mind about the book, perhaps because someone else has just published a very similar book or they think the market has moved on, think carefully about what you do. It's important to weigh up all the aspects. Is the publisher right? Has the market changed and the book's place disappeared? Has something happened in the market to take away the chance that it'll get bought?

Trying to understand why the publisher is taking this action is essential if you are to make the right decision about what to do. Though the first temptation is to try and force them to publish, it's not always the best course of action. Think: if the publisher has been forced into publishing a book they don't want to publish, are they going to do a good job of it? I don't think so either. It may be better to insist that you are allowed to keep the advance (or receive a payment in lieu of royalties that you will not now receive) and make sure you get something in writing to say that all rights in the book have now reverted back to you (immediately). If the market has truly gone away, you might want to cut your losses and accept it. If not, then you are free to go and sell it somewhere else, to somebody who wants it.

What to do if your publisher doesn't like the manuscript you deliver

Generally you can expect some feedback and probably some revision. If your editor is any good, they will probably suggest some changes. In 10 years, the number of manuscripts I have passed without scribbling on them at least moderately I can count on one hand. More than a few I've asked for fairly substantial rewrites. Editors are usually really aware that having your pride and joy scribbled on can be hard to take. We do, really. There are some manuscripts that I send feedback on with a really heavy heart, as I am so concerned about how the author will take it. Editors honestly don't get the red pen out for fun, we do it because we are trying to make your manuscript as good as it possibly can be. We do it because we want your book to sell – for both our sakes.

It is always worth remembering however that it's a hell of a lot easier to write all over something than it is to write the thing in the first place. Some editors are aware of this and are quite humble. Others realise just how much easier it is to rewrite than to write only if they experience being an author themselves.

Be prepared for feedback and be prepared to be asked for revisions. Be as open as you can possibly be to this. If your editor is good, then the feedback should be useful and constructive. If you really strongly disagree with the feedback, then talk to your editor about it. In my experience it's very rare for there to be a major issue at this point. It's usually a case of agreeing what to do to address any concerns the editor may have and do some fine tuning.

Worst case scenario time

Very, very rarely, an editor will go back to the author and tell them the book has been rejected. Is unpublishable. Has been refused on the grounds of quality. Isn't what was asked for and agreed. Whatever the reason given, in the very unlikely event this happens, try to stay calm. This is not necessarily the end of the world. The first thing to do is to ask the editor to be very explicit about exactly what is wrong. You need to get them to do this in writing, so that you can take it in and consider it carefully. If you don't understand, then go back to the editor and explain that you don't understand.

If you can see what the editor is getting at, and think you can address the concerns and would like to, then ask if that's possible. This should only be attempted at first with a small sample of the book, as you don't want to waste hours rewriting if it's not going to work anyway. It's very likely the editor will agree to this, as there's nothing for them to lose except the time it takes them to look at the revised book.

However, if you don't understand or accept the reasons given, then there are two possible explanations:

1. There is a mismatch in what you have written and what the editor wanted, but you can't see it.

2. Something else is going on that you don't know about.

The latter sounds rather like a conspiracy theory, so I'll give you a real example to illustrate that though extremely rare, it can happen:

> "I wrote a non-fiction book for a smallish but well established publisher. My original submission had included an outline and three full chapters and I was offered a contract pretty sharpish with little discussion. I finished the rest of the book, eight chapters in total, and submitted it to the publisher well before the deadline. A couple of days later, I received a letter that I couldn't believe. They had rejected the book completely and the letter contained a litany of my offences including not conforming to scope, unacceptable quality, and so on. It just didn't seem possible – they had offered me a contract on the basis of three chapters, I'd done the other five along exactly the lines of the sample chapters and as set out in the outline. How could they reject it? I went to my then agent in a very confused state. He didn't look at all surprised and told me not to worry, they had obviously run out of money again. He suggested what I did was wait, change a few bits, and resubmit it in a month's time. I did exactly as he said, changing only the order of a couple of chapters and altering the first lines. It was accepted immediately without com-

ment, was duly published and sold very nicely indeed. I still have the rejection letter on my wall. I'd never write for them again."
Roger, full time author

I couldn't quite believe this story, but the letter exists to prove it – and the author I know well. It's true. Roger has written dozens of books and this is the only time this has ever happened to him, so it is a very rare occurrence. Though I would never work for a company that asked me to do this, it does illustrate that publishing companies with the morals of an alley cat, and people willing to work for them, do exist. You do have to consider the possibility that something might be going on that you don't know about. This is the reason that it always makes sense to ask if you can remedy any shortcomings and resubmit in a month or so. You can then eliminate the possibility that this was about to happen to you.

Far more likely is the possibility that there is a mismatch between what you have written and what the editor wanted. Even if you can't see it. For them to not want to publish the book and not to believe the faults can be remedied, it has to be a fairly serious mismatch. If they are taking are firm stance or if you have tried to remedy the book to their satisfaction but haven't been able to, then there are really only two courses of action you can now take:

1 Try and force the publisher to publish.

2 Accept that the publisher doesn't want the book and try to place it elsewhere.

If you have an outline and sample material that you both agreed, and you believe that your manuscript corresponds to this, then you can insist the publisher honour their contractual obligation to publish. In some cases, even if the publisher doesn't agree that you've produced the manuscript to acceptable standards of scope and quality, they may opt to back down rather than have a protracted battle over it (knowing a battle could be expensive legally and in time and resources – and costly in bad PR terms also). However we've already established that there's little point trying to force a publisher to publish against their will.

Better for you, better for the publisher and better for the book would be to try and place it elsewhere. This is especially true if you've had a go at revising it and it hasn't worked out. Consider talking to the publisher and suggesting that you will take it away and pitch to other publishers, and ask that you keep your advance on the understanding that if you do place it elsewhere, you will pay the advance back.

If the idea for the book was yours, then morally it's entirely fair for you to take it elsewhere. If the idea came from the publisher, you should ask if it's acceptable for you to do this. It's the decent thing to do.

There's no doubt the rejection is horribly painful at this stage – far worse than at proposal stage, but remember that all publishers see joy in different things and that one publisher's reject could be another publisher's bestseller.

If you don't manage to place it elsewhere, you can always self publish with the advance of the first publisher (if they've allowed you to keep it). Or maybe, just maybe, this book didn't work out and you can learn from it and move on.

What if the copy editor does an overzealous job and you don't like it?

Oh dear. Another one that does occur from time to time. The copy editor has been a bit too handy with the red pen. Maybe the copy editor feels they have to do something to justify their existence. Or you might simply disagree with their changes. Don't get in a state over it. Speak to your editorial contact first of all (the person overseeing the passage of your manuscript through editing and production). Tell them what you are annoyed or upset about and wait for them to suggest a solution. If it's not forthcoming, tell them what you'd like to be done about it. Chances are if you explain yourself well, the editorial person will see the problem and sort it out. If they side with the copy editor, speak to your commissioning editor.

What to do if you are sick or injured or your circumstances change and you can't complete your book on time

This happens too. One author of mine had a skiing accident and broke all his ribs. He couldn't sit at a computer for months afterwards. It'll give your editor a major headache but they have to deal with it so be honest and tell them everything as early as you can. If they can, they will hold out for you (or I would hope they would). If the book is your idea, morally they should, if it's at all possible. If it was the publisher's idea and it's very deadline sensitive, you might have to accept that somebody else will have to finish the job. Maybe you could have some input into who that is and oversee them?

Special notes on highly illustrated publishing

Highly illustrated books are 'design led' – pages are designed ready for text to be added according to a preset layout. For the author, this means that even if you write exactly the right amount of words asked of you, they will be edited (in a process known as 'cut and fill') if they don't fit the allotted space exactly. The editor either removes words or adds a few extra words in to make the text fit the number of lines exactly. However, you might not like what they've done and this could be tough, as although you should be allowed to change anything you don't like at page proofs, you may not always see final changes, much less get a change to alter them. Alternatively, some publishers will ask you to do the cut and fill yourself (literally 'lose eight words here' and the like), in which case you keep control but it will be fiddly and boring.

Staying the right side of the law

In Chapter 7, we looked at the contractual obligations that you have agreed to in respect of using other people's copyrighted material and ensuring you don't break the law (for example by writing something libellous). Bear this in mind while you write, and if you are in any doubt whatsoever, flag what you've done with your publisher and ask for advice.

Working with your publisher after publication

So, the moment you've been waiting for has arrived. Your printed and bound copies arrive. Your book is really a book. And very shortly it will be officially published. Doesn't this book end here? Well, yes and no. Technically yes, because your book is published. But no, because your role in working with the publisher isn't over.

You can of course kick back and relax and wait to see your book fly off the shelves. However, what you do now can have a significant impact on how well your book sells. And after getting this far, surely you want to do all you can to make sure it does sell?

Here are 10 ways you can help ensure your book gets off to the best possible start:

1 Speaking

Opportunities to speak in public expose you to a new audience. This is great for your book. It's not for everybody, but increasing your profile as an author will help raise awareness of your book. 'Self-marketing' in this way really helps.

2 News/feature articles

Will your local media do a feature on you? Can you contribute a feature article to local press or specialist national press if relevant? The 'local woman has first children's book published' normally carries some interest – and of course you can use it with local bookstores to raise your profile that way.

3 Help the in house publicity team

Most larger publishers have one or more in house publicists. Others use freelances. However, rarely does a publisher have enough in the way of PR resources to do the fullest and best possible job on every title. If you can help support their PR effort, you can really make a difference. Always ask the in house team what you can do to help, rather than demanding to know why your book hasn't been reviewed in *The Times* yet.

4 Ask stores if you can sign copies

Wherever you go, pop into the bookstores and ask the staff if they would like you to sign any copies of your book they happen to have. If you're lucky, the staff will highlight your book then as 'signed copies'.

5 Befriend booksellers

I know people who have done this to great effect. I don't mean the head office staff, I mean the person in your local branch of whatever bookstore. If they know you and your book, they might keep a watch on it and make sure they always have stock. It definitely never hurts.

6 Befriend reps

This one isn't always easy, but the sales reps of your publisher (or distributor) have a lot of books to sell. If you can engineer a way of meeting them, or getting on their radar, your book may benefit.

Golden rule

Whatever you do in trying to get to meet reps and other publishing staff, don't become a pest. Make sure what you do is in the mind-set of what you can do for them, not what they can do for you.

---

7 Get to know as many people in house as you can

This is related to point 6 above. The more people know and like you, the more likely they are to think of your book.

8 Raise your book's profile on amazon

If you know somebody who has read your book and likes it, ask if they will write a review on amazon to say so. Some authors buy a few copies of their own book from amazon to raise the sales ranking and hope it gets noticed by more people that way. Ask relevant people who like your book if they will put their list of favourite books on 'listmania' and include yours in it. Drive people from your website to amazon to buy your book, just by clicking – and ask other website owners if they will plug your book too.

9 Build a great website

This is especially relevant if yours is a non-fiction book on a particular subject. Say it's a book on horse care, if you build a website about buying and looking after horses, you can not only promote your own book, but become known as a potential speaker and build your profile that way.

10 Use your network

Starting a word of mouth campaign can be very powerful. People tend to read books that are recommended to them. The more you can get people talking about your book the better. If it's a young children's book, can you give a copy to the local nursery and tell them who you are and that you'd like their feedback. If it's a novel, can you seek out the local reading group and ask if they'd be interested in your book (give them copies to start with)? If it's a book about starting a business, can you ask your local enterprise agency if they can recommend it?

9 Dealing with rejection

How to learn from the knockbacks

'I'm sorry to say that your book does not fit our list, at present, and we will therefore be unable to take it on for publication.' Ouch. Not again. The much loathed rejection slip or letter arrives, delivering the most hurtful of paper cuts. So what do you do now?

Dealing with rejection isn't just about deciding whether or not to burn the letters or keep them for posterity. Nor is it about me delivering words of platitude. It's about seeing if you can glean anything from the response of the agent or publisher that will help you work out whether you need to change something in your approach. It's possible that you might need to rethink the kind of person or company you are approaching, change what you say, or accept that maybe the publishers are all right, and this isn't an idea that's going to work commercially.

Then again, it might be that this particular submission didn't light the fire of this particular agent or editor, and you just need to try again with somebody else.

Whatever the reason, rejection is brutal. Agents and editors don't enjoy rejecting submissions, unless the author has been particularly annoying in the way they made the approach. There may be a mild sense of relief as the pile of submissions on the desk gets one submission shorter, I admit. But that's not personal. Remember that agents and editors start out wanting your proposal to be great.

You have to find a way of letting the rejection go, but learning from it if you can. Maybe you can use it as a driver to prove the agent or editor wrong. However you tackle it mentally, you should also remember that one rejection doth not a failure make.

I can't help but start with my favourite rejection story.

Case in point

Two authors came to me one day to discuss a book proposal they had sent in about how to turn a good idea into a great business. I really liked it. I thought it was original, very well written and was a cut above most of the rather dry books I'd seen on the subject. After I had told them all the good news, and that I'd like to publish the book, the co-authors seemed delighted out of proportion to the news. Surely, I thought, they know it's good? It turned out that the reason for their joy was that immediately before coming to see me, the pair had been to see one of my biggest competitors, where they had been told that not only were they not going to get an offer, but the book was 'unpublishable'. I published the 'unpublishable', with only minor revisions, it went straight into the bestseller charts and triggered hundreds of emails from readers about how useful the book is. It's now in its second edition.

This is a personal account – of course there are dozens of stories of bestselling books for which the authors have a collection of rejection slips. Despite securing a good agent on her second attempt, JK Rowling was rejected by some of the biggest publishing houses. The total number of publishers who it is claimed turned down *Harry Potter* varies between three and 12, but I'll use Jo's own words from her website: lots.

So, if and when your book submission is turned down, here's a quick list of things to run through:

1. Just because one editor, agent or reader doesn't like it, it doesn't mean that all will feel the same way. It's decision making at its most subjective. It's not a science.
2. Just because one publishing house didn't want it, it doesn't mean all will feel the same way. All publishers have slightly differing preferences and a different set of books on their list. Some will be limited by the numbers of books they can publish in any year, others publish unlimited numbers, some have profitability targets for individual books that mean yours might not work for them, others will accept a lower return on investment. The variables are considerable.
3. Just because one agent didn't want the book, it doesn't mean nobody will want to represent you. There are as many different types of agent as there are types of book.
4. Does the rejection give a reason why? Does this make any sense to you? Can you glean anything useful from it, either about you and your book or about the publisher?

5 Are you sure what you've sent is well written and that your idea is commercially sound? Is there anything you need to do to change either of these aspects?

Reasons you might be given for rejection – and what they mean

When you hear back from a publisher or agent (if you hear back at all), you may get a 'thanks but no thanks' kind of note, or you may get some kind of explanation. The explanation may be true and therefore useful. Then again it might not. You see, nice publishers and agents feel a kind of obligation to give authors a reason for the rejection; however there are things they can't or won't say, and sometimes there's just no reason at all other than that they simply didn't like it.

I'd love to do a 'what they say and what they mean' list here but it would be a bit trite, so instead I will give you some common real reasons for rejection:

1 The writing was bad.

2 The book had no structure.

3 Your particular storyline or style didn't appeal to the editor/agent.

4 The editor or agent doesn't believe there's a market for the book.

5 The editor already has a book on that subject and doesn't want another.

6 The book falls in a genre that was popular but isn't any more.

7 There's too much competition that's too good.

8 You came across badly as an author.

9 Your submission was carelessly worded or presented.

10 The editor or agent didn't agree with your premise.

There are endless others.

The main point here is that many books are rejected on the basis of a gut reaction. As one insider put it "The answer is no. Anything else is hot air."

So what do you do with the rejection information? If there seems to be something genuinely constructive in the rejection, then use it if you think it will help and it makes sense to you.

However, for fiction, children's books and poetry in particular, the best advice seems to be: don't change it completely just on the basis of one person's preference. Try and find somebody who likes it as it is.

And for non-fiction: if the market isn't big enough for a big publisher, try a smaller one.

Should you ever ask for more feedback?

When you've had a rejection, you might be tempted to go back and ask for feedback. Especially if you've just had a standard one liner. If you do ask, then two things to remember:

1 Don't expect an answer. The editor or agent will probably simply not have enough time to be able to explain their full thinking to you, even if they can or are willing to. You can of course get feedback from a critique or editorial service company, where you pay for a full and frank opinion.

2 In the unlikely event you do get an answer, it may be hard to take. The editor or agent may have given you a polite rejection, alluding to the broad general reasons, but if you persist and they do reply, it could be fairly damning.

Feedback is a double-edged sword. If somebody tells you that you can't write for toffee and should give up, then it could be true (in which case useful), but then again, it could be just that person's opinion and others wouldn't agree.

When to give up

So how many publishers or agents or both do you try before you finally give up? Really this is down to you, and how determined you are, and to your belief in your book. If you are sure your book is truly publishable (are you being really honest with yourself?), then persistence is vital.

> "Exhaust the market before you give up if you really believe in it. It only takes one person to say yes."
> *Laura James, journalist and author*

If you've been targeting agents, think about trying a small publisher directly instead. If you've been targeting small publishers, consider an agent for the bigger ones that won't accept your submission without one. Only you know when to give up.

Confidence boosters

Here are a few thoughts to keep you going and help you work out if anything needs to be changed:

1 Remember publishers *need* good authors.

2 Be yourself. Don't pretend to be something or someone you aren't.

3 Your book is a commodity – have you made it as saleable as possible?

4 Think about how you like to be sold to. Is there anything there that suggests you should change your approach?

5 Have you been confident and positive? If you don't believe in your book, others are unlikely to.

6 Have you made life as easy as possible for the publisher or agent? What else could you do?

Should you ever argue with a rejection?

The simple answer is no. You might be surprised how many authors – and even agents – do. One editor told me that it drives her crazy when agents argue with her rejection of a book, "I've already said no, I'm not going to change my mind, so there's no point!" It's worse as an editor being argued with by an agent, as they should know better, but as an author it's equally pointless to argue with either agent or editor. Agents have been known to be stalked by rejected authors – anybody who argues back tends to make people distinctly nervous.

The only time I would advise going back to a publisher after they've rejected your book is if you have additional information to support your case that you haven't previously shared with them. For example, if you were able to guarantee a sale of the book, or a really big name had agreed to endorse it.

Arguing is almost always futile. Gut feeling plays such a huge part in deciding whether or not to take on a book, and you really can't argue with a gut feeling. And for heaven's sake, never ever waste your time with a response like 'You clearly haven't understood my proposal – please read it again.' There's no win in this situation. Leave it. Move on. Get over it!

10 Self publishing

How to publish your own book (with or without help)

Self publishing used to have an image problem. Suddenly, it's becoming quite cool – the association with 'vanity publishing' is wearing off and it's definitely experiencing a surge in popularity. I even hear of authors who tell me they chose to self publish – a far cry from its previous standing as the last refuge of the failure.

> "Do it yourself publishing has become the new route to success for struggling authors. Several have recently won lucrative contracts from the biggest publishers after proving the worth of their books by first printing them themselves and selling them in local bookshops. The falling cost of self publishing means that authors whose work has been turned down by literary agents or publishers are now able to prove that their books will sell."
> *Danuta Kean in the* Sunday Telegraph

However, it's not simply that there are more would-be authors who are just happy to see their book in print and don't mind the DIY approach to getting there. One of the reasons for the greater interest in self publishing is that it is now seen as a step towards a proper publishing deal. Increasingly, it can be a way of standing out of the slush pile and getting your book noticed by the big houses.

I've definitely seen an increase in recent years in the number of self published books sent to me by people looking for that elusive publishing deal. And like many publishers, I've taken one or two on. It doesn't mean I've accepted the book exactly as self published – on the contrary, I am as happy to deconstruct an actual book and rework it into what I want as I am a manuscript, though not all publishers feel the same. But having a physical book in my hands and the evidence that the author has already sold 500 copies on their own, can make it a fairly impressive book proposal.

A couple of warnings

Be warned that a bad manuscript self published becomes a bad book. Do not kid yourself that just having it properly typeset and bound will make it more attractive as a publishing proposition if it's poor quality writing, an ill thought through proposition, or a book in search of a market.

The other major warning is related to the cost. Self publishing is not cheap. It could easily set you back several thousand pounds. If you are looking at self publishing as an investment, with the intention of making money from it, then be very, very careful. If this is your reasoning then you should look at it like any business proposition and get some firm sales lined up before you invest your money. No sensible person would start a business before they had fully tested the market for their product and ideally lined up more than one customer. The same is true if you're looking to make money from self publishing. Just because your mum/partner/friends say they like your book doesn't mean you'll be able to sell any.

If you can afford to lose a couple of thousand pounds, then by all means take a risk if you want to. If not, make sure you have customers and sales outlets lined up, or you could end up seriously out of pocket.

Self publishing options

If you're willing to put your own cash behind getting your book published, then you have two main options:

1. Use some or all of the services of a self publishing agency.
2. Do it all entirely yourself. If you've got the energy and the time, you can do everything yourself, bringing in a designer, copy editor and proofreader (maybe even indexer) yourself and liaise personally with printers and binders.

Advantages to self publishing

1. You are in control. You can create exactly the book you want – inside and out.
2. If all you want is to have your book in print, and money's no object, it's perfect.
3. It's a way of getting your book noticed by the big publishers. As book submissions go, you don't get much better presented than this.
4. It shows a would-be publisher that you are driven, determined, that you will market yourself and your book – and most importantly, it shows them that the sales are there. If you can walk into a publisher telling them that your local Ottakers took 10 copies and sold them all in a month, you have an advantage. It's free road testing for the publisher.

The downsides to self publishing

1 Money

It's expensive. You will have to pay everything up front and there's no nice advance to tide you over. You are taking all the financial risk of the project, on top of which you can get ripped off if you don't know what you're doing.

2 Sales and distribution

If you want your book to be available in most stores, you'll struggle to do it yourself. The biggest mistake people make when they decide to self publish is to think only about producing the actual book itself. What they forget or don't realise, is that this is only half of the publishing story. The other half is the getting people to stock the book and make it available for sale. Many retailers don't even see smaller publishers, never mind a self published person with one book. The best you can hope for is to manage to get the book listed on amazon, and copies in your local shops.

3 Lack of professional input

Publishers make it look deceptively easy. You could make all the mistakes in the publishing game without realising it.

4 Hard work

It's very time consuming handling everything yourself, from type-setting and cover design to dealing with printers and finding customers. Even if you use a self publishing company, you still need to be prepared to invest time in the whole process.

5 It might not help you get a contract with a publisher at all

In the same way that you should never send a full manuscript for a non-fiction book to a publisher, if the editor sees a self published book as a fait accompli, they may be put off as their chance to help shape it is gone (or made harder).

DIY or use a service provider?

It is entirely possible to self publish a book without using a self publishing company. It's a bit more work, but you are then completely in control. If you know what you are doing, or are a shrewd negotiator, you could do well to do it this way. Even if you don't know what you're doing, the learning experience can be fun (I know several people who have done it and really enjoyed it). The big drawback is that unless you can persuade a distributor to hold stock of the book and supply orders, you will find yourself doing all the back office stuff yourself. And that can be a big effort. However, some self publishers don't do much in the way of selling in any case.

Case in point

Jill Paton Walsh self published a novel which was later shortlisted for the Booker Prize. The decision to self publish *Knowledge of Angels* was taken after failing to find a publisher. A publishing house later picked it up. Despite having had such success, she is circumspect about taking that route:

"The first rule is: *only do it as a last resort.*

The second is: don't risk more money than you can afford to lose." says Jill.[1]

[1] For more advice on self publishing from Paton Walsh, see **www.greenbay.co.uk/advice**

Five good reasons to think about self publishing

1 You know it's probably not going to be a commercially viable book for a big publisher – eg a local history book.

2 You only want a limited number of copies for your own use – eg a family related book – but you want it to be professionally done for posterity.

3 You know you can sell a lot of books yourself and aren't worried about whether or not it's available in bookshops. An example might be if you are a small business with lots of clients, or a charity for people with a rare condition with all the contacts you need to reach the market.

4 It's a first-to-market opportunity and you can't wait for a publisher to decide and act.

5 If a mainstream publisher has turned you down, you want to prove there is a market for your book and you are confident you can do it.

"My experience may not be typical because I had an agent and a publisher beforehand and I had found these people with relative ease. However, the agent was sadly afflicted with narcolepsy and our relationship ended after one year and (I would estimate) about three or four hours of work on her part to pitch my book. I did not have the heart or the patience to look for another agent. The first publisher I approached was a very small and enthusiastic outfit, but I soon realised that the editor did not understand my book or its market, and when they announced they were going ahead with a truly ridiculous cover for my book, I knew I had to get free. Another year wasted. But why self publish? The short answer is that I felt extremely fed up at the time and thought 'If they're all going to be like this then I might as well do it myself'."

Cheryl Walmsley, author, Your Future Looks Bright. *Her self published edition has now been picked up and republished by a large publisher.*

Two dubious reasons for deciding to self publish

1 I'll make more money this way.

True, you will make more money per copy, probably, but only if you print the exact number you can sell and don't end up with wasted stock (in which case your profits go out of the window as the cost per copy is high). And of course it goes without saying that a publishing company is likely to sell far more copies than you can. If you've got an offer from a publisher, it's likely to pay to take it.

2 Who needs a publisher anyway? I'm cutting out the middle man.

Ah that old chestnut. It's so easy to underestimate what goes into producing a high quality book. And even if you do manage to clear the hurdles on quality of editing, design, layout, proofing and printing, there's the Beecher's Brook of getting into shops. Every author I have ever spoken to who has self published said they had no idea how difficult it would be even to get their book listed on amazon, never mind get copies into any physical store.

Vanity publishing

Vanity publishing and self publishing are not the same thing. The vanity publisher publishes your book under their imprint – just like a normal publisher, except they ask you to pay them to do it.

Of course, it's never put quite like that when vanity publishers advertise for new clients. And here's a key word: advertise. No genuine normal publisher advertises for authors. (They don't have to – remember good publishers are besieged with authors offering proposals and manuscripts.) Vanity publishers on the other hand advertise in the back of national newspapers with rallying cries such as 'Authors Wanted!'. They tell you sometimes that they are asking for a 'contribution' towards publication or refer to themselves as 'subsidy publishers' or 'partner publishers'. The bottom line is that you are paying them to publish your book.

The cost will be anything from about £2,500 to £10,000 or more, depending on the type of book. You may be promised a huge royalty – up to 30%, which is three times what a traditional publisher would pay – however, it normally comes with a proviso that you sell a certain number of copies first.

And here's where the real snag comes. Since you have actually paid the company to publish the book for you, they have invested absolutely nothing in the book themselves. So they have absolutely no reason to try and sell a single copy of the book for you. Whatever they say. Chances are, if there's any selling to be done, it'll be down to you.

Many people have had very bad experiences of vanity publishing, as even if the actual book itself is passably produced (and it often isn't), you'll probably never see a copy in a shop ever.

Vanity publishing versus self publishing

A much better, and much cheaper, option is to use the services of a self publishing company, where you can pick what services you need, and you direct the whole operation. You are the publisher in this scenario, not the company. You are simply buying in services from the company, according to what you want and need.

However, if you want to opt for a 'complete package' from a self publisher, given the ability of vanity publishers to market themselves creatively, how do you tell the difference?

Here are four ways to identify a genuine self publishing service company (as opposed to a vanity publisher)

1 Ask for recommendations. A genuine self publishing service company should be able to provide you with the names of authors whose books they have produced. Ask if you can be put in contact with a couple of the people. If the company is genuine, there's no reason they wouldn't agree. They might want to ask the other authors for permission to put you in touch of course.

2 With a list of some of the books and authors provided, check if these books are available on amazon. If they are, and are under different 'publisher' names, then they should be self published not vanity published.

3 Does the company issue your book with an ISBN? Do they supply the main libraries with copies? An ISBN means the book can be sold by retailers. Without it, you are looking at a vanity publication.

4 Will they allow you to have your own 'publishing house' name on the book? A self publish company will always let you have your own publisher brand on the book, not theirs.

The fees of self publishing service companies can vary quite substantially, from as little as £600 to as much as £3,000 for pretty much the same service. It definitely pays to shop around and get quotes. The biggest part of the overall cost is likely to be for the actual printing and binding of copies. A small print run (say 500 copies or so) makes it very expensive per copy. However, there's no point getting a better deal by ordering more if you are never going to need or sell them. Many companies now offer 'Print on Demand' (POD) which means that copies are digitally printed (rather than on a printing press) and you can order only one copy at a time. The quality is not bad at all – in fact many professional publishers now make use of POD for books that are selling a handful of copies a year but that they don't want to put out of print. It's also known as Available on Demand (AOD).

The Society of Authors offers advice on vanity publishing and self publishing – in particular they suggest being very wary of paying any company for any deal where your book is published online, as an e-book, or as POD only. The cost to the publisher is very low, but the chances are they will do little other than list your book on a website. You can be sure they won't sell many – and worse still part of the deal may tie you in to giving that publisher a share of any future earnings if it does get properly published. As yet, e-books haven't really taken off for mainstream publishers, so you can be certain that vanity publishing websites won't sell many. If you want to test the market with an e-book then the best bet is to set up your own basic website and sell it or make it available there. That way you are in control.

DIY self publishing

If you don't want to use the services of a self publishing company, you can of course opt to take the complete DIY approach. It simply requires you have the time and mindset to learn as you go, read everything you can on the subject, ask lots of questions and shop around for people whose services you absolutely have to buy in (printing would be one of these). If you are thinking about this route, I would strongly recommend you buy and read one of the books on the subject (sadly there isn't room here for me to explain everything you need to do to publish a book), use the internet for research and if possible see what you can learn from people who have been there before you – there's lots of useful guidance in the resources section to accompany this book at **www.whiteladderpress.com**, plus a full account of one author's self publishing experience.

Conclusion

Whether you decide to approach a publisher or agent, large company or small; whether you opt for self publishing or decide to set up a publishing company of your own; whether you keep writing and submitting at a prolific rate or conclude that actually you really aren't too bothered about being published at all, I hope this book has been useful.

As I said from the outset, publishing isn't a science, and nor is getting published. In places I've had to intentionally avoid a prolonged debate – some of the topics could have become whole books in their own right. I'd be genuinely pleased to hear what you liked about the book and what you think would improve it in future editions. Do drop me a line: **rachael@stockanderson.com**.

Above all else, enjoy what you do. Writing should be a pleasure. Good luck!

Index